# AIR FRYER CHICKEN WINGS

## OVER 100 DELICIOUS AND HEALTHY RECIPES

# *Air Fryer Chicken Wings*

13-Digit ISBN: 978-1-64643-056-7
10-Digit ISBN: 1-64643-056-5

This book may be ordered by mail from the publisher. Please include $5.99 for postage and handling. Please support your local bookseller first!

Books published by Cider Mill Press Book Publishers are available at special discounts for bulk purchases in the United States by corporations, institutions, and other organizations. For more information, please contact the publisher.

Cider Mill Press Book Publishers
"Where good books are ready for press"
PO Box 454
12 Spring Street
Kennebunkport, Maine 04046
Visit us online! www.cidermillpress.com

Typography: Sentinel, Bushcraft, Helvetica Rounded
All photos are used under official license from Shutterstock.com
Back cover image: Sesame Chicken Wings, see page 71.

Printed in China
1 2 3 4 5 6 7 8 9 0
First Edition

# AIR FRYER CHICKEN WINGS

## OVER 100 DELICIOUS AND HEALTHY RECIPES

CIDER MILL PRESS

BOOK PUBLISHERS

KENNEBUNKPORT, MAINE

# *Contents*

**NOTE:** DEPENDING ON WHAT MODEL AIR FRYER YOU HAVE, YOU MAY NEED TO SPLIT THE CHICKEN WINGS AT THEIR JOINTS IN ORDER TO FIT THEM IN THE BASKET AND PROVIDE THEM WITH THE SPACE NEEDED TO PRODUCE THE DESIRED RESULT.

# *Introduction*

In a short amount of time, the air fryer has become a beloved, if not essential, part of the home kitchen. Its rapid preheating faculty, efficiency, and even circulation of heat make cooking a breeze, and the air fryer's compact size and ability to be cleaned quickly make it an ideal counter to the frequently cluttered and time-constrained state of contemporary life.

While those are desirable qualities in any appliance, the air fryer's value is most apparent in the food it turns out. Crispy, crunchy, and almost unbelievably light due to the limited amount of cooking fat it requires, the air fryer manages to provide all of the treasured attributes of deep-fried foods while managing to avoid the downsides.

And while it is capable of elevating a number of foods, it seems to many that the air fryer was made for the chicken wing. Simply put, no other food shines quite so bright when exposed to the air fryer's abilities. The rich flavors you typically have to venture away from the homestead for are now available in minutes, and there's no need to concern yourself with the danger and grease that deep frying at home comes with.

Something as sublime as air-fried chicken wings calls out for a tome that is devoted to helping them soar even higher. Taking that as a cue, we've gone around the globe and come back with rubs, marinades, and sauces that capture the world's most cherished flavors and make the most of chicken's notoriously neutral taste. We also, for those times when you want something more than a quick snack, gathered a number of delicious, wholesome side dishes to help you round out your plate—and reduce any potential guilt.

# *There's the Rub*

Throwing together various spices and applying the mixture to chicken wings is one of the easiest, and most effective, ways to enhance the flavor of your favorite treats. Composed almost exclusively with items common to every pantry, you can be certain you'll find something that satisfies any craving.

## INGREDIENTS

1 tablespoon allspice

2 teaspoons dried thyme

1¼ teaspoons curry powder

2 teaspoons paprika

1¼ teaspoons sugar

1 teaspoon kosher salt

1 teaspoon black pepper

1 tablespoon cayenne pepper

½ teaspoon grated fresh nutmeg

½ teaspoon cinnamon

¼ teaspoon ground cloves

2 lbs. chicken wings

# Wings with Jamaican Jerk Rub

**YIELD: 6 SERVINGS • ACTIVE TIME: 10 MINUTES**
**TOTAL TIME: 40 MINUTES**

The island's most famous flavor packs quite a punch.

*1.* Spray the air fryer's basket with cooking spray and set it aside. Place all of the ingredients, except for the chicken wings, in a mixing bowl and stir until combined.

*2.* Pat the chicken wings dry. Either toss the wings in the rub until they are evenly coated, or apply it by hand.

*3.* Place the wings in the basket so that they are not touching. Set the air fryer to 360°F and cook for 12 minutes. Turn the chicken wings over and cook for another 12 minutes. Raise the heat to 390°F, cook until the wings are extremely crispy, about 6 minutes, and serve.

# Southwestern Wings

YIELD: 6 SERVINGS • ACTIVE TIME: 10 MINUTES
TOTAL TIME: 40 MINUTES

The earthy, smoky flavors the Southwest is famed for are an ideal match for chicken wings.

## INGREDIENTS

1 tablespoon chili powder

1 tablespoon paprika

2 teaspoons cayenne pepper

2 teaspoons cumin

2 teaspoons coriander

1 garlic clove, minced

2 teaspoons kosher salt

2 teaspoons black pepper

2 lbs. chicken wings

1. Spray the air fryer's basket with cooking spray and set it aside. Place all of the ingredients, except for the chicken wings, in a mixing bowl and stir until combined.

2. Pat the chicken wings dry. Either toss the wings in the rub until they are evenly coated, or apply it by hand.

3. Place the wings in the basket so that they are not touching. Set the air fryer to 360°F and cook for 12 minutes. Turn the chicken wings over and cook for another 12 minutes. Raise the heat to 390°F, cook until the wings are extremely crispy, about 6 minutes, and serve.

# Berbere Chicken Wings

**YIELD: 6 SERVINGS • ACTIVE TIME: 10 MINUTES
TOTAL TIME: 40 MINUTES**

Berbere is an Ethiopian spice mix that is incredibly versatile—be sure to try it on more than just wings.

*1.* Spray the air fryer's basket with cooking spray and set it aside. Place all of the ingredients, except for the chicken wings, in a mixing bowl and stir until combined.

*2.* Pat the chicken wings dry. Either toss the wings in the rub until they are evenly coated, or apply it by hand.

*3.* Place the wings in the basket so that they are not touching. Set the air fryer to 360°F and cook for 12 minutes. Turn the chicken wings over and cook for another 12 minutes. Raise the heat to 390°F, cook until the wings are extremely crispy, about 6 minutes, and serve.

## INGREDIENTS

2 teaspoons ground fenugreek

2 teaspoons red pepper flakes

2½ tablespoons paprika

1 teaspoon cardamom

1 teaspoon ground nutmeg

¼ teaspoon garlic powder

¼ teaspoon ground cloves

¼ teaspoon cinnamon

¼ teaspoon allspice

2 lbs. chicken wings

# Chicken Wings with Rustic Pepper Rub

YIELD: 6 SERVINGS • ACTIVE TIME: 10 MINUTES
TOTAL TIME: 40 MINUTES

A trio of peppers proves to be the magic number.

## INGREDIENTS

2 garlic cloves, minced

2 teaspoons finely chopped fresh thyme

2 teaspoons kosher salt

1½ teaspoons black pepper

1½ teaspoons white pepper

1 teaspoon cayenne pepper

1 teaspoon paprika

½ teaspoon onion powder

2 lbs. chicken wings

1. Spray the air fryer's basket with cooking spray and set it aside. Place all of the ingredients, except for the chicken wings, in a mixing bowl and stir until combined.

2. Pat the chicken wings dry. Either toss the wings in the bowl until they are evenly coated, or apply the rub by hand.

3. Place the wings in the basket so that they are not touching. Set the air fryer to 360°F and cook for 12 minutes. Turn the chicken wings over and cook for another 12 minutes. Raise the heat to 390°F, cook until the wings are extremely crispy, about 6 minutes, and serve.

There's the Rub 17

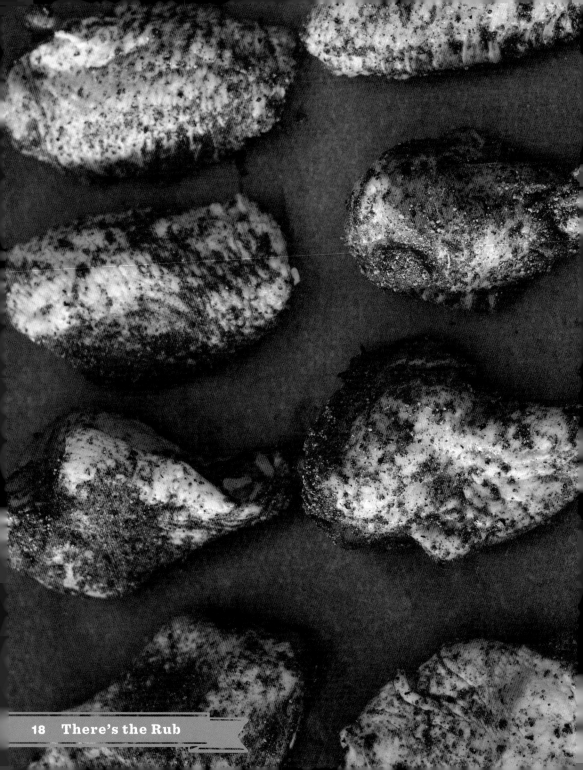

# St. Louis Chicken Wings

**YIELD: 6 SERVINGS • ACTIVE TIME: 10 MINUTES**
**TOTAL TIME: 40 MINUTES**

The paprika beautifully bridges the gap between the spice of the ground ginger and mustard powder and the sweetness of the brown sugar.

*1.* Spray the air fryer's basket with cooking spray and set it aside. Place all of the ingredients, except for the chicken wings, in a mixing bowl and stir until combined.

*2.* Pat the chicken wings dry. Either toss the wings in the rub until they are evenly coated, or apply it by hand.

*3.* Place the wings in the basket so that they are not touching. Set the air fryer to 360°F and cook for 12 minutes. Turn the chicken wings over and cook for another 12 minutes. Raise the heat to 390°F, cook until the wings are extremely crispy, about 6 minutes, and serve.

### INGREDIENTS

1 tablespoon sweet paprika

2 teaspoons garlic powder

2 teaspoons black pepper

2 teaspoons kosher salt

2 teaspoons onion powder

2 teaspoons dark brown sugar

2 teaspoons ground ginger

2 teaspoons mustard powder

½ teaspoon celery salt

2 lbs. chicken wings

# Smoked Paprika Chicken Wings

**YIELD: 6 SERVINGS • ACTIVE TIME: 10 MINUTES**
**TOTAL TIME: 40 MINUTES**

A rich, smoky rub that is sure to delight.

### INGREDIENTS

2 tablespoons smoked paprika

2 teaspoons coriander

2 teaspoons cumin

1 teaspoon cayenne pepper

1 tablespoon black pepper

1 tablespoon kosher salt

2 lbs. chicken wings

*1.* Spray the air fryer's basket with cooking spray and set it aside. Place all of the ingredients, except for the chicken wings, in a mixing bowl and stir until combined.

*2.* Pat the chicken wings dry. Either toss the wings in the rub until they are evenly coated, or apply it by hand.

*3.* Place the wings in the basket so that they are not touching. Set the air fryer to 360°F and cook for 12 minutes. Turn the chicken wings over and cook for another 12 minutes. Raise the heat to 390°F, cook until the wings are extremely crispy, about 6 minutes, and serve.

# Spicy Cinnamon Chicken Wings

**YIELD: 6 SERVINGS • ACTIVE TIME: 10 MINUTES
TOTAL TIME: 40 MINUTES**

Even in this crowded field of spices, cinnamon manages to stand out.

*1.* Spray the air fryer's basket with cooking spray and set it aside. Place all of the ingredients, except for the chicken wings, in a mixing bowl and stir until combined.

*2.* Pat the chicken wings dry. Either toss the wings in the rub until they are evenly coated, or apply it by hand.

*3.* Place the wings in the basket so that they are not touching. Set the air fryer to 360°F and cook for 12 minutes. Turn the chicken wings over and cook for another 12 minutes. Raise the heat to 390°F, cook until the wings are extremely crispy, about 6 minutes, and serve.

## INGREDIENTS

1½ teaspoons paprika

1 tablespoon garlic powder

1½ teaspoons mustard powder

1½ teaspoons ancho chili powder

1½ teaspoons onion powder

1½ teaspoons black pepper

1½ teaspoons kosher salt

1 teaspoon cinnamon

½ teaspoon cumin

2 lbs. chicken wings

# *Ancho Chili Chicken Wings*

**YIELD: 6 SERVINGS • ACTIVE TIME: 10 MINUTES
TOTAL TIME: 40 MINUTES**

While you may think that this is a very hot rub, it is actually relatively mild, and almost sweet.

## INGREDIENTS

1 tablespoon paprika

2 teaspoons ancho chili powder

2 teaspoons coriander

2 teaspoons cumin

1 teaspoon dried oregano

2 teaspoons allspice

1 teaspoon onion powder

½ teaspoon cinnamon

2 lbs. chicken wings

1. Spray the air fryer's basket with cooking spray and set it aside. Place all of the ingredients, except for the chicken wings, in a mixing bowl and stir until combined.

2. Pat the chicken wings dry. Either toss the wings in the rub until they are evenly coated, or apply it by hand.

3. Place the wings in the basket so that they are not touching. Set the air fryer to 360°F and cook for 12 minutes. Turn the chicken wings over and cook for another 12 minutes. Raise the heat to 390°F, cook until the wings are extremely crispy, about 6 minutes, and serve.

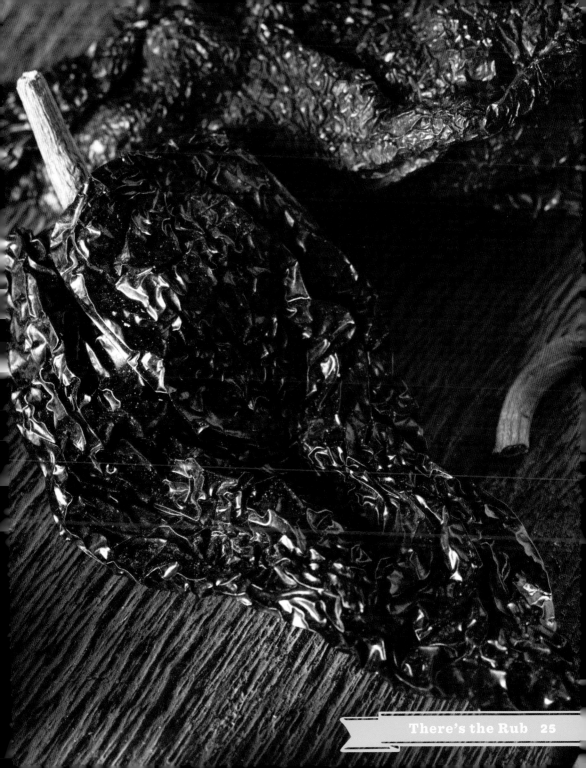

# Smoky & Spicy Wings

**YIELD: 6 SERVINGS • ACTIVE TIME: 10 MINUTES**
**TOTAL TIME: 40 MINUTES**

The chipotle does the heavy lifting in this wonderful mix.

*1.* Spray the air fryer's basket with cooking spray and set it aside. Place all of the ingredients, except for the chicken wings, in a mixing bowl and stir until combined.

*2.* Pat the chicken wings dry. Either toss the wings in the rub until they are evenly coated, or apply it by hand.

*3.* Place the wings in the basket so that they are not touching. Set the air fryer to 360°F and cook for 12 minutes. Turn the chicken wings over and cook for another 12 minutes. Raise the heat to 390°F, cook until the wings are extremely crispy, about 6 minutes, and serve.

## INGREDIENTS

1½ tablespoons smoked paprika

1½ tablespoons black pepper

2 teaspoons chipotle chili powder

1 tablespoon chili powder

1½ teaspoons cayenne pepper

½ teaspoon cumin

½ teaspoon dried oregano

Salt, to taste

2 lbs. chicken wings

# Chicken Wings with Dukkah

**YIELD: 6 SERVINGS • ACTIVE TIME: 10 MINUTES**
**TOTAL TIME: 40 MINUTES**

A popular Middle Eastern blend of spices, seeds, and nuts, dukkah makes for a memorable wing.

*1.* Place a large, dry cast-iron skillet over medium heat and add all of the ingredients other than the salt and chicken wings. Toast, while stirring continuously, until the seeds and nuts are lightly browned.

*2.* Remove from heat and use a mortar and pestle or a spice grinder to grind the mixture into a powder. Make sure to not grind the mixture too much, as you do not want it to become a paste. Add the salt and stir to incorporate.

*3.* Spray the air fryer's basket with cooking spray and pat the chicken wings dry. Either toss the wings in the rub until they are evenly coated, or apply the rub by hand.

*4.* Place the wings in the basket so that they are not touching. Set the air fryer to 360°F and cook for 12 minutes. Turn the chicken wings over and cook for another 12 minutes. Raise the heat to 390°F, cook until the wings are extremely crispy, about 6 minutes, and serve.

## INGREDIENTS

1 tablespoon pumpkin seeds

1 tablespoon hazelnuts or pistachios

1 tablespoon peanuts

½ teaspoon black peppercorns

1½ teaspoons white sesame seeds

½ teaspoon dried mint

1½ teaspoons finely chopped fresh thyme

½ teaspoon coriander seeds

½ teaspoon cumin seeds

1 teaspoon kosher salt

2 lbs. chicken wings

# Sweet & Spicy Chicken Wings

**YIELD: 6 SERVINGS • ACTIVE TIME: 10 MINUTES**
**TOTAL TIME: 40 MINUTES**

Don't hesitate to tweak the amount of mustard powder used here, as its pleasant tang goes a long way.

*1.* Spray the air fryer's basket with cooking spray and set it aside. Place all of the ingredients, except for the chicken wings, in a mixing bowl and stir until combined.

*2.* Pat the chicken wings dry. Either toss the wings in the rub until they are evenly coated, or apply it by hand.

*3.* Place the wings in the basket so that they are not touching. Set the air fryer to 360°F and cook for 12 minutes. Turn the chicken wings over and cook for another 12 minutes. Raise the heat to 390°F, cook until the wings are extremely crispy, about 6 minutes, and serve.

## INGREDIENTS

3 tablespoons ancho chili powder

2 teaspoons paprika

1 teaspoon black pepper

1 teaspoon kosher salt

½ teaspoon cumin

½ teaspoon cayenne pepper

1 teaspoon mustard powder

½ teaspoon dried oregano

2 lbs. chicken wings

# Punjabi Wings

**YIELD: 6 SERVINGS • ACTIVE TIME: 10 MINUTES**
**TOTAL TIME: 40 MINUTES**

The flavors that power the famous samosa exact their charms on succulent chicken wings to equally memorable results.

## INGREDIENTS

1 teaspoon coriander seeds, crushed

½ teaspoon fennel seeds, crushed

Pinch of fenugreek seeds, crushed

1-inch piece of fresh ginger, peeled and minced

1 garlic clove, minced

1 teaspoon minced jalapeño pepper

1 teaspoon chili powder

1 tablespoon coriander

¾ teaspoon turmeric

1½ teaspoons amchoor powder

½ teaspoon garam masala

2 lbs. chicken wings

*1.* Spray the air fryer's basket with cooking spray and set it aside. Place all of the ingredients, except for the chicken wings, in a mixing bowl and stir until combined.

*2.* Pat the chicken wings dry. Either toss the wings in the rub until they are evenly coated, or apply it by hand.

*3.* Place the wings in the basket so that they are not touching. Set the air fryer to 360°F and cook for 12 minutes. Turn the chicken wings over and cook for another 12 minutes. Raise the heat to 390°F, cook until the wings are extremely crispy, about 6 minutes, and serve.

# Cajun Chicken Wings

**YIELD: 6 SERVINGS • ACTIVE TIME: 10 MINUTES
TOTAL TIME: 40 MINUTES**

Salty, spicy, and plenty savory, this rub infuses your wings with the culinary genius of Louisiana.

*1.* Spray the air fryer's basket with cooking spray and set it aside. Place all of the ingredients, except for the chicken wings, in a mixing bowl and stir until combined.

*2.* Pat the chicken wings dry. Either toss the wings in the rub until they are evenly coated, or apply it by hand.

*3.* Place the wings in the basket so that they are not touching. Set the air fryer to 360°F and cook for 12 minutes. Turn the chicken wings over and cook for another 12 minutes. Raise the heat to 390°F, cook until the wings are extremely crispy, about 6 minutes, and serve.

### INGREDIENTS

2 tablespoons kosher salt

1 tablespoon black pepper

1½ teaspoons paprika

1½ teaspoons garlic powder

1 teaspoon onion powder

1 teaspoon cayenne pepper

1 teaspoon dried thyme

2 lbs. chicken wings

# Smoky Cajun Chicken Wings

**YIELD: 6 SERVINGS • ACTIVE TIME: 10 MINUTES
TOTAL TIME: 40 MINUTES**

Lovers of smoke get all they can handle here.

### INGREDIENTS

2 tablespoons kosher salt

1 tablespoon black pepper

1½ teaspoons smoked paprika

1½ teaspoons garlic powder

1 teaspoon onion powder

1 teaspoon cayenne pepper

1 teaspoon dried thyme

1 teaspoon liquid smoke

2 lbs. chicken wings

*1.* Spray the air fryer's basket with cooking spray and set it aside. Place all of the ingredients, except for the chicken wings, in a mixing bowl and stir until combined.

*2.* Pat the chicken wings dry. Either toss the wings in the rub until they are evenly coated, or apply it by hand.

*3.* Place the wings in the basket so that they are not touching. Set the air fryer to 360°F and cook for 12 minutes. Turn the chicken wings over and cook for another 12 minutes. Raise the heat to 390°F, cook until the wings are extremely crispy, about 6 minutes, and serve.

# Rosemary Chicken Wings

**YIELD: 6 SERVINGS • ACTIVE TIME: 10 MINUTES
TOTAL TIME: 40 MINUTES**

Few things lift chicken wings to greater heights than fresh herbs.

*1.* Spray the air fryer's basket with cooking spray and set it aside. Place all of the ingredients, except for the chicken wings and olive oil, in a mixing bowl and stir until combined.

*2.* Pat the chicken wings dry and rub them with the olive oil. Either toss the wings in the rub until they are evenly coated, or apply it by hand.

*3.* Place the wings in the basket so that they are not touching. Set the air fryer to 360°F and cook for 12 minutes. Turn the chicken wings over and cook for another 12 minutes. Raise the heat to 390°F, cook until the wings are extremely crispy, about 6 minutes, and serve.

## INGREDIENTS

2 tablespoons finely chopped fresh parsley

2 tablespoons finely chopped fresh rosemary

2 garlic cloves, minced

1½ teaspoons black pepper

1½ teaspoons kosher salt

2 lbs. chicken wings

2 tablespoons olive oil

# Wings with Coffee Rub

**YIELD: 6 SERVINGS • ACTIVE TIME: 10 MINUTES**
**TOTAL TIME: 40 MINUTES**

The bitterness of the coffee cuts wonderfully against the sweet brown sugar.

## INGREDIENTS

1½ tablespoons finely ground coffee

2 teaspoons dark brown sugar

2 teaspoons garlic powder

2 teaspoons paprika

2 teaspoons onion powder

1½ teaspoons cumin

1½ teaspoons kosher salt

2 lbs. chicken wings

1. Spray the air fryer's basket with cooking spray and set it aside. Place all of the ingredients, except for the chicken wings, in a mixing bowl and stir until combined.

2. Pat the chicken wings dry. Either toss the wings in the rub until they are evenly coated, or apply it by hand.

3. Place the wings in the basket so that they are not touching. Set the air fryer to 360°F and cook for 12 minutes. Turn the chicken wings over and cook for another 12 minutes. Raise the heat to 390°F, cook until the wings are extremely crispy, about 6 minutes, and serve.

## INGREDIENTS

2 teaspoons finely
ground coffee

½ teaspoon coriander

2 teaspoons black pepper

Pinch of red pepper flakes

¼ teaspoon cumin

½ teaspoon mustard powder

½ teaspoon dark chili powder

¼ teaspoon paprika

2 tablespoons kosher salt

2 tablespoons
light brown sugar

2 lbs. chicken wings

# Wings with Sweet & Spicy Coffee Rub

**YIELD: 6 SERVINGS • ACTIVE TIME: 10 MINUTES**
**TOTAL TIME: 40 MINUTES**

Adding a little spice to a coffee-based rub is a surefire way to get people's attention.

*1.* Spray the air fryer's basket with cooking spray and set it aside. Place all of the ingredients, except for the chicken wings, in a mixing bowl and stir until combined.

*2.* Pat the chicken wings dry. Either toss the wings in the rub until they are evenly coated, or apply it by hand.

*3.* Place the wings in the basket so that they are not touching. Set the air fryer to 360°F and cook for 12 minutes. Turn the chicken wings over and cook for another 12 minutes. Raise the heat to 390°F, cook until the wings are extremely crispy, about 6 minutes, and serve.

# Curry Chicken Wings

**YIELD: 6 SERVINGS • ACTIVE TIME: 10 MINUTES
TOTAL TIME: 40 MINUTES**

As people all over the world are well aware, curry and chicken were made for each other.

**INGREDIENTS**

1 tablespoon curry powder

1½ teaspoons smoked paprika

1½ teaspoons ground ginger

1 teaspoon cumin

1 teaspoon allspice

1 teaspoon black pepper

½ teaspoon kosher salt

2 lbs. chicken wings

*1.* Spray the air fryer's basket with cooking spray and set it aside. Place all of the ingredients, except for the chicken wings, in a mixing bowl and stir until combined.

*2.* Pat the chicken wings dry. Either toss the wings in the rub until they are evenly coated, or apply it by hand.

*3.* Place the wings in the basket so that they are not touching. Set the air fryer to 360°F and cook for 12 minutes. Turn the chicken wings over and cook for another 12 minutes. Raise the heat to 390°F, cook until the wings are extremely crispy, about 6 minutes, and serve.

# Smoky Lemon-Pepper Wings

**YIELD: 6 SERVINGS • ACTIVE TIME: 10 MINUTES**
**TOTAL TIME: 40 MINUTES**

A tremendous spin on a stone-cold classic wing flavoring.

1. Spray the air fryer's basket with cooking spray and set it aside. Place all of the ingredients, except for the chicken wings, in a mixing bowl and stir until combined.

2. Pat the chicken wings dry. Either toss the wings in the rub until they are evenly coated, or apply it by hand.

3. Place the wings in the basket so that they are not touching. Set the air fryer to 360°F and cook for 12 minutes. Turn the chicken wings over and cook for another 12 minutes. Raise the heat to 390°F, cook until the wings are extremely crispy, about 6 minutes, and serve.

### INGREDIENTS

1 tablespoon smoked paprika

1 tablespoon black pepper

1 teaspoon dried basil

1 teaspoon dried tarragon

¼ teaspoon garlic powder

1 teaspoon lemon zest

½ teaspoon chili powder

½ teaspoon onion powder

2 lbs. chicken wings

# Chili & Cumin Wings

YIELD: 6 SERVINGS • ACTIVE TIME: 10 MINUTES
TOTAL TIME: 40 MINUTES

It may make a few eyes water, but for fans of heat this rub can't be beat.

## INGREDIENTS

1½ tablespoons chili powder

1½ tablespoons smoked paprika

2 teaspoons dried oregano

1 teaspoon cumin

1 teaspoon black pepper

1 teaspoon kosher salt

½ teaspoon dried thyme

2 lbs. chicken wings

1. Spray the air fryer's basket with cooking spray and set it aside. Place all of the ingredients, except for the chicken wings, in a mixing bowl and stir until combined.

2. Pat the chicken wings dry. Either toss the wings in the rub until they are evenly coated, or apply it by hand.

3. Place the wings in the basket so that they are not touching. Set the air fryer to 360°F and cook for 12 minutes. Turn the chicken wings over and cook for another 12 minutes. Raise the heat to 390°F, cook until the wings are extremely crispy, about 6 minutes, and serve.

# Wings with Dill & Coriander Rub

**YIELD: 6 SERVINGS • ACTIVE TIME: 10 MINUTES**
**TOTAL TIME: 40 MINUTES**

The aroma lent by the fresh dill makes these wings easy to linger over with a cold beer or two.

*1.* Spray the air fryer's basket with cooking spray and set it aside. Place all of the ingredients, except for the chicken wings and olive oil, in a mixing bowl and stir until combined.

*2.* Pat the chicken wings dry and coat them with the olive oil. Either toss the wings in the rub until they are evenly coated, or apply it by hand.

*3.* Place the wings in the basket so that they are not touching. Set the air fryer to 360°F and cook for 12 minutes. Turn the chicken wings over and cook for another 12 minutes. Raise the heat to 390°F, cook until the wings are extremely crispy, about 6 minutes, and serve.

## INGREDIENTS

1½ tablespoons black pepper

1½ tablespoons coriander seeds, crushed

1 tablespoon finely chopped fresh dill

2 garlic cloves, minced

1 tablespoon kosher salt

1 teaspoon paprika

2 lbs. chicken wings

2 tablespoons olive oil

# *Wings with BBQ Rub*

**YIELD: 6 SERVINGS • ACTIVE TIME: 10 MINUTES**
**TOTAL TIME: 40 MINUTES**

No grill is no problem with this rub in tow.

### INGREDIENTS

1 tablespoon brown sugar

1 tablespoon sweet paprika

1 teaspoon onion powder

1 teaspoon dried oregano

1 teaspoon dried savory

1 teaspoon cayenne pepper

½ teaspoon garlic powder

1 tablespoon kosher salt

1½ teaspoons black pepper

2 lbs. chicken wings

*1.* Spray the air fryer's basket with cooking spray and set it aside. Place all of the ingredients, except for the chicken wings, in a mixing bowl and stir until combined.

*2.* Pat the chicken wings dry. Either toss the wings in the rub until they are evenly coated, or apply it by hand.

*3.* Place the wings in the basket so that they are not touching. Set the air fryer to 360°F and cook for 12 minutes. Turn the chicken wings over and cook for another 12 minutes. Raise the heat to 390°F, cook until the wings are extremely crispy, about 6 minutes, and serve.

# Cayenne Chicken Wings

**YIELD: 6 SERVINGS • ACTIVE TIME: 10 MINUTES**
**TOTAL TIME: 40 MINUTES**

These spicy wings would be perfect beside some of the Coconut & Cucumber Salad on page 207.

*1.* Spray the air fryer's basket with cooking spray and set it aside. Place all of the ingredients, except for the chicken wings, in a mixing bowl and stir until combined.

*2.* Pat the chicken wings dry. Either toss the wings in the rub until they are evenly coated, or apply it by hand.

*3.* Place the wings in the basket so that they are not touching. Set the air fryer to 360°F and cook for 12 minutes. Turn the chicken wings over and cook for another 12 minutes. Raise the heat to 390°F, cook until the wings are extremely crispy, about 6 minutes, and serve.

### INGREDIENTS

1 tablespoon celery salt

1 tablespoon cayenne pepper

2 teaspoons paprika

2 teaspoons allspice

1 tablespoon black pepper

1 tablespoon kosher salt

2 lbs. chicken wings

# Chipotle Chicken Wings

YIELD: 6 SERVINGS • ACTIVE TIME: 10 MINUTES
TOTAL TIME: 40 MINUTES

Essentially, chipotles are smoked jalapeños, so if you're a fan of heat, don't hesitate to toss another pepper into this rub.

## INGREDIENTS

2 dried chipotle peppers, seeded and minced

1 tablespoon dried oregano

1 tablespoon dried cilantro

1 tablespoon black pepper

2 teaspoons cumin

1 teaspoon onion powder

½ teaspoon mustard powder

½ teaspoon kosher salt

2 lbs. chicken wings

1. Spray the air fryer's basket with cooking spray and set it aside. Place all of the ingredients, except for the chicken wings, in a mixing bowl and stir until combined.

2. Pat the chicken wings dry. Either toss the wings in the rub until they are evenly coated, or apply it by hand.

3. Place the wings in the basket so that they are not touching. Set the air fryer to 360°F and cook for 12 minutes. Turn the chicken wings over and cook for another 12 minutes. Raise the heat to 390°F, cook until the wings are extremely crispy, about 6 minutes, and serve.

# Wings with Herb & Garlic Rub

**YIELD: 6 SERVINGS • ACTIVE TIME: 10 MINUTES
TOTAL TIME: 40 MINUTES**

These wings provide a whirlwind tour of Mediterranean flavors.

*1.* Spray the air fryer's basket with cooking spray and set it aside. Place all of the ingredients, except for the chicken wings and olive oil, in a mixing bowl and stir until combined.

*2.* Pat the chicken wings dry and coat them with the olive oil. Either toss the wings in the rub until they are evenly coated, or apply it by hand.

*3.* Place the wings in the basket so that they are not touching. Set the air fryer to 360°F and cook for 12 minutes. Turn the chicken wings over and cook for another 12 minutes. Raise the heat to 390°F, cook until the wings are extremely crispy, about 6 minutes, and serve.

### INGREDIENTS

1 tablespoon finely chopped fresh oregano

2 garlic cloves, minced

2 tablespoons finely chopped fresh thyme

2 teaspoons black pepper

1 teaspoon kosher salt

1 teaspoon cumin

1 teaspoon coriander

2 lbs. chicken wings

2 tablespoons olive oil

# Wings with Fennel & Coriander Rub

**YIELD: 6 SERVINGS • ACTIVE TIME: 10 MINUTES
TOTAL TIME: 40 MINUTES**

The most straightforward rub in the book, meaning it is as close to actual perfection as is possible.

*1.* Spray the air fryer's basket with cooking spray and set it aside. Place the seeds in a dry skillet and toast over medium heat, shaking the skillet frequently, until they are fragrant, about 2 minutes. Remove from heat and grind the seeds with a mortar and pestle or a spice grinder. Stir in the salt and pepper.

*2.* Pat the chicken wings dry. Either toss the wings in the rub until they are evenly coated, or apply it by hand.

*3.* Place the wings in the basket so that they are not touching. Set the air fryer to 360°F and cook for 12 minutes. Turn the chicken wings over and cook for another 12 minutes. Raise the heat to 390°F, cook until the wings are extremely crispy, about 6 minutes, and serve.

2 tablespoons fennel seeds

1 tablespoon coriander
seeds

2 teaspoons black pepper

2 teaspoons kosher salt

2 lbs. chicken wings

# Rosemary & Thyme Wings

**YIELD: 6 SERVINGS • ACTIVE TIME: 10 MINUTES**
**TOTAL TIME: 40 MINUTES**

It doesn't get top billing, but the lemon zest is what makes this rub work.

*1.* Spray the air fryer's basket with cooking spray and set it aside. Place all of the ingredients, except for the chicken wings and olive oil, in a mixing bowl and stir until combined.

*2.* Pat the chicken wings dry and coat them with the olive oil. Either toss the wings in the rub until they are evenly coated, or apply it by hand.

*3.* Place the wings in the basket so that they are not touching. Set the air fryer to 360°F and cook for 12 minutes. Turn the chicken wings over and cook for another 12 minutes. Raise the heat to 390°F, cook until the wings are extremely crispy, about 6 minutes, and serve.

## INGREDIENTS

2 garlic cloves, minced

2 tablespoons finely chopped fresh rosemary

1 tablespoon finely chopped fresh thyme

1 tablespoon ground black pepper

2 teaspoons kosher salt

1 teaspoon lemon zest

2 lbs. chicken wings

2 tablespoons olive oil

# Coriander & Paprika Wings

YIELD: 6 SERVINGS • ACTIVE TIME: 10 MINUTES
TOTAL TIME: 40 MINUTES

The citrusy, nutty flavor of coriander is vastly underutilized. This rub makes efforts to remedy that.

## INGREDIENTS

1 tablespoon coriander

1½ teaspoons black pepper

½ teaspoon mustard powder

1 tablespoon kosher salt

1 teaspoon garlic powder

1 teaspoon onion powder

1½ teaspoons dark brown sugar

1 tablespoon sweet paprika

2 lbs. chicken wings

*1.* Spray the air fryer's basket with cooking spray and set it aside. Place all of the ingredients, except for the chicken wings, in a mixing bowl and stir until combined.

*2.* Pat the chicken wings dry. Either toss the wings in the bowl until they are evenly coated, or apply the rub by hand.

*3.* Place the wings in the basket so that they are not touching. Set the air fryer to 360°F and cook for 12 minutes. Turn the chicken wings over and cook for another 12 minutes. Raise the heat to 390°F, cook until the wings are extremely crispy, about 6 minutes, and serve.

# Wings with Five-Spice Rub

**YIELD: 6 SERVINGS • ACTIVE TIME: 10 MINUTES**
**TOTAL TIME: 40 MINUTES**

The flavors that make up the popular Chinese spice blend also make for an outstanding rub.

*1.* Spray the air fryer's basket with cooking spray and set it aside. Place all of the ingredients, except for the chicken wings, in a mixing bowl and stir until combined.

*2.* Pat the chicken wings dry. Either toss the wings in the rub until they are evenly coated, or apply it by hand.

*3.* Place the wings in the basket so that they are not touching. Set the air fryer to 360°F and cook for 12 minutes. Turn the chicken wings over and cook for another 12 minutes. Raise the heat to 390°F, cook until the wings are extremely crispy, about 6 minutes, and serve.

## INGREDIENTS

2 teaspoons ground star anise

2 teaspoons cinnamon

2 teaspoons Sichuan pepper

2 teaspoons ground fennel

2 teaspoons ground cloves

2 teaspoons garlic powder

2 teaspoons ground ginger

2 teaspoons kosher salt

2 lbs. chicken wings

# Ancho & Paprika Wings

**YIELD: 6 SERVINGS • ACTIVE TIME: 10 MINUTES**
**TOTAL TIME: 40 MINUTES**

The bit of heat from the red pepper flakes is a welcome addition amidst all this sweetness.

## INGREDIENTS

1 tablespoon sweet paprika

1 tablespoon ancho chili powder

1 teaspoon garlic powder

1 tablespoon black pepper

1 tablespoon kosher salt

1 teaspoon dried oregano

1 teaspoon red pepper flakes

2 lbs. chicken wings

1. Spray the air fryer's basket with cooking spray and set it aside. Place all of the ingredients, except for the chicken wings, in a mixing bowl and stir until combined.

2. Pat the chicken wings dry. Either toss the wings in the rub until they are evenly coated, or apply it by hand.

3. Place the wings in the basket so that they are not touching. Set the air fryer to 360°F and cook for 12 minutes. Turn the chicken wings over and cook for another 12 minutes. Raise the heat to 390°F, cook until the wings are extremely crispy, about 6 minutes, and serve.

# Marinate on It

A marinade requires patience. If you have a hunger for wings that needs to be satisfied ASAP, you'll have to look elsewhere in this book. But the time required by a marinade carries two massive advantages: your chicken wings get infused with incredible flavor, and you suddenly have the flexibility needed to navigate your busy life, since you don't have to choose between preparing something delicious and getting stuff done.

# Sesame Chicken Wings

**YIELD: 6 SERVINGS • ACTIVE TIME: 20 MINUTES**
**TOTAL TIME: 2 HOURS AND 45 MINUTES**

The takeout favorite, now in the comfort of your home.

*1.* Place all of the ingredients, except for the chicken wings, in a mixing bowl or a plastic bag and stir until combined. Place the chicken wings in the marinade and chill in the refrigerator for at least 2 hours, stirring or shaking occasionally.

*2.* Remove the chicken wings from the refrigerator, remove them from the marinade, and shake to remove any excess. Spray the air fryer's basket with cooking spray and set it aside.

*3.* Place the wings in the basket so that they are not touching. Set the air fryer to 360°F and cook for 12 minutes. Turn the chicken wings over and cook for another 12 minutes. Raise the heat to 390°F, cook until the wings are extremely crispy, about 6 minutes, and serve.

### INGREDIENTS

½ cup olive oil

2 tablespoons sesame oil

2-inch piece of fresh ginger, peeled and minced

2 scallions, trimmed and minced

4 garlic cloves, minced

Juice of 1 lemon

Salt and pepper, to taste

3 tablespoons sesame seeds

3 tablespoons honey

2 lbs. chicken wings

# Apple & Herb Chicken Wings

**YIELD: 6 SERVINGS • ACTIVE TIME: 20 MINUTES**
**TOTAL TIME: 2 HOURS AND 45 MINUTES**

Moist, succulent wings are assured thanks to the apple cider.

### INGREDIENTS

2 cups fresh apple cider

¼ cup olive oil

Juice from ½ lemon

2 sprigs of fresh thyme

2 sprigs of fresh rosemary

2 garlic cloves, minced

1 tablespoon black pepper

2 teaspoons kosher salt

2 lbs. chicken wings

*1.* Place all of the ingredients, except for the chicken wings, in a mixing bowl or a plastic bag and stir until combined. Place the chicken wings in the marinade and chill in the refrigerator for at least 2 hours, stirring or shaking occasionally.

*2.* Remove the chicken wings from the refrigerator, remove them from the marinade, and shake to remove any excess. Spray the air fryer's basket with cooking spray and set it aside.

*3.* Place the wings in the basket so that they are not touching. Set the air fryer to 360°F and cook for 12 minutes. Turn the chicken wings over and cook for another 12 minutes. Raise the heat to 390°F, cook until the wings are extremely crispy, about 6 minutes, and serve.

# Wings in Red Wine & Basil Marinade

**YIELD: 6 SERVINGS • ACTIVE TIME: 20 MINUTES**
**TOTAL TIME: 2 HOURS AND 45 MINUTES**

Pinot Noir or Merlot are strong choices if you're searching for a wine to use in this marinade.

**1.** Place all of the ingredients, except for the chicken wings, in a mixing bowl or a plastic bag and stir until combined. Place the chicken wings in the marinade and chill in the refrigerator for at least 2 hours, stirring or shaking occasionally.

**2.** Remove the chicken wings from the refrigerator, remove them from the marinade, and shake to remove any excess. Spray the air fryer's basket with cooking spray and set it aside.

**3.** Place the wings in the basket so that they are not touching. Set the air fryer to 360°F and cook for 12 minutes. Turn the chicken wings over and cook for another 12 minutes. Raise the heat to 390°F, cook until the wings are extremely crispy, about 6 minutes, and serve.

### INGREDIENTS

2 cups fresh basil leaves, finely chopped

2 large carrots, peeled and minced

2 large yellow onions, minced

2 garlic cloves, minced

2 sprigs of fresh thyme

2 sprigs of fresh rosemary

2 sprigs of fresh oregano

3 tablespoons olive oil

2 cups dry red wine

2 lbs. chicken wings

# Citrus & Sage Chicken Wings

**YIELD: 6 SERVINGS • ACTIVE TIME: 20 MINUTES**
**TOTAL TIME: 2 HOURS AND 45 MINUTES**

The earthy flavor of fresh sage is brightened considerably by the addition of citrus.

1. Place all of the ingredients, except for the chicken wings, in a mixing bowl or a plastic bag and stir until combined. Place the chicken wings in the marinade and chill in the refrigerator for at least 2 hours, stirring or shaking occasionally.

2. Remove the chicken wings from the refrigerator, remove them from the marinade, and shake to remove any excess. Spray the air fryer's basket with cooking spray and set it aside.

3. Place the wings in the basket so that they are not touching. Set the air fryer to 360°F and cook for 12 minutes. Turn the chicken wings over and cook for another 12 minutes. Raise the heat to 390°F, cook until the wings are extremely crispy, about 6 minutes, and serve.

### INGREDIENTS

3 garlic cloves, chopped

⅓ cup fresh sage

Zest and juice of 3 oranges

1 tablespoon coriander

½ tablespoon black pepper

½ teaspoon red pepper flakes

¼ cup olive oil

1 tablespoon kosher salt

1 shallot, chopped

2 lbs. chicken wings

# Teriyaki Chicken Wings

**YIELD: 6 SERVINGS • ACTIVE TIME: 20 MINUTES**
**TOTAL TIME: 2 HOURS AND 45 MINUTES**

Teriyaki: everyone knows it, and everyone loves it.

## INGREDIENTS

½ cup soy sauce

¼ cup brown sugar

2 tablespoons rice vinegar

2 garlic cloves, chopped

1-inch piece of fresh ginger, peeled and chopped

1 teaspoon black pepper

2 lbs. chicken wings

*1.* Place all of the ingredients, except for the chicken wings, in a mixing bowl or a plastic bag and stir until combined. Place the chicken wings in the marinade and chill in the refrigerator for at least 2 hours, stirring or shaking occasionally.

*2.* Remove the chicken wings from the refrigerator, remove them from the marinade, and shake to remove any excess. Spray the air fryer's basket with cooking spray and set it aside.

*3.* Place the wings in the basket so that they are not touching. Set the air fryer to 360°F and cook for 12 minutes. Turn the chicken wings over and cook for another 12 minutes. Raise the heat to 390°F, cook until the wings are extremely crispy, about 6 minutes, and serve.

# Garlic & Herb Wings

**YIELD: 6 SERVINGS • ACTIVE TIME: 20 MINUTES
TOTAL TIME: 2 HOURS AND 45 MINUTES**

Any fresh herb can be swapped in for the members of this trio.

*1.* Place all of the ingredients, except for the chicken wings, in a mixing bowl or a plastic bag and stir until combined. Place the chicken wings in the marinade and chill in the refrigerator for at least 2 hours, stirring or shaking occasionally.

*2.* Remove the chicken wings from the refrigerator, remove them from the marinade, and shake to remove any excess. Spray the air fryer's basket with cooking spray and set it aside.

*3.* Place the wings in the basket so that they are not touching. Set the air fryer to 360°F and cook for 12 minutes. Turn the chicken wings over and cook for another 12 minutes. Raise the heat to 390°F, cook until the wings are extremely crispy, about 6 minutes, and serve.

## INGREDIENTS

3 garlic cloves, crushed

1 sprig of fresh rosemary

1 sprig of fresh thyme

2 bay leaves

2 cups olive oil

1 tablespoon black pepper

1 tablespoon kosher salt

2 lbs. chicken wings

# Wings in Red Wine & Dijon Marinade

**YIELD: 6 SERVINGS • ACTIVE TIME: 20 MINUTES**
**TOTAL TIME: 2 HOURS AND 45 MINUTES**

This rich marinade helps you make the most of chicken's famously mild flavor.

*1.* Place all of the ingredients, except for the chicken wings, in a mixing bowl or a plastic bag and stir until combined. Place the chicken wings in the marinade and chill in the refrigerator for at least 2 hours, stirring or shaking occasionally.

*2.* Remove the chicken wings from the refrigerator, remove them from the marinade, and shake to remove any excess. Spray the air fryer's basket with cooking spray and set it aside.

*3.* Place the wings in the basket so that they are not touching. Set the air fryer to 360°F and cook for 12 minutes. Turn the chicken wings over and cook for another 12 minutes. Raise the heat to 390°F, cook until the wings are extremely crispy, about 6 minutes, and serve.

## INGREDIENTS

1¾ cups dry red wine

¼ cup olive oil

2 garlic cloves, chopped

2 tablespoons Dijon
mustard

1 tablespoon black pepper

1 tablespoon kosher salt

1 sprig of fresh rosemary

2 lbs. chicken wings

# Garlic & Lemon Chicken Wings

Some may think this is too much garlic, but the lemon juice ensures that everything's just right.

1. Place all of the ingredients, except for the chicken wings, in a mixing bowl or a plastic bag and stir until combined. Place the chicken wings in the marinade and chill in the refrigerator for at least 2 hours, stirring or shaking occasionally.

2. Remove the chicken wings from the refrigerator, remove them from the marinade, and shake to remove any excess. Spray the air fryer's basket with cooking spray and set it aside.

3. Place the wings in the basket so that they are not touching. Set the air fryer to 360°F and cook for 12 minutes. Turn the chicken wings over and cook for another 12 minutes. Raise the heat to 390°F, cook until the wings are extremely crispy, about 6 minutes, and serve.

## INGREDIENTS

Juice from 4 lemons

2 tablespoons olive oil

6 garlic cloves, chopped

3 sprigs of fresh rosemary

1 teaspoon ground fennel

1 tablespoon black pepper

1 tablespoon kosher salt

2 lbs. chicken wings

# Pineapple Chicken Wings

**YIELD: 6 SERVINGS • ACTIVE TIME: 20 MINUTES**
**TOTAL TIME: 2 HOURS AND 45 MINUTES**

Any remaining residue will firm up in the air fryer, coating the chicken wings with a pleasant glaze.

## INGREDIENTS

1½ cups pineapple juice

¼ cup brown sugar

¼ cup soy sauce

2 garlic cloves, chopped

1 teaspoon kosher salt

2 lbs. chicken wings

1. Place all of the ingredients, except for the chicken wings, in a mixing bowl or a plastic bag and stir until combined. Place the chicken wings in the marinade and chill in the refrigerator for at least 2 hours, stirring or shaking occasionally.

2. Remove the chicken wings from the refrigerator, remove them from the marinade, and shake to remove any excess. Spray the air fryer's basket with cooking spray and set it aside.

3. Place the wings in the basket so that they are not touching. Set the air fryer to 360°F and cook for 12 minutes. Turn the chicken wings over and cook for another 12 minutes. Raise the heat to 390°F, cook until the wings are extremely crispy, about 6 minutes, and serve.

## INGREDIENTS

½ cup chicken stock

½ cup soy sauce

½ cup mirin

¼ cup sake

½ cup brown sugar

2 garlic cloves, crushed

1-inch piece of fresh
ginger, peeled and sliced

1½ scallions, trimmed
and sliced

2 lbs. chicken wings

# Tare Chicken Wings

**YIELD: 6 SERVINGS • ACTIVE TIME: 20 MINUTES**
**TOTAL TIME: 2 HOURS AND 45 MINUTES**

Think of this marinade as a thicker, more flavorful version of teriyaki.

*1.* Place all of the ingredients, except for the chicken wings, in a small saucepan and bring to a simmer over medium heat. Reduce heat to medium-low and simmer, stirring once or twice, until the mixture has reduced slightly, about 10 minutes. Remove from heat and let cool completely.

*2.* Place the marinade in a mixing bowl or a plastic bag. Place the chicken wings in the marinade and chill in the refrigerator for at least 2 hours, stirring or shaking occasionally.

*3.* Remove the chicken wings from the refrigerator, remove them from the marinade, and shake to remove any excess. Spray the air fryer's basket with cooking spray and set it aside.

*4.* Place the wings in the basket so that they are not touching. Set the air fryer to 360°F and cook for 12 minutes. Turn the chicken wings over and cook for another 12 minutes. Raise the heat to 390°F, cook until the wings are extremely crispy, about 6 minutes, and serve.

# Balsamic Wings

**YIELD: 6 SERVINGS • ACTIVE TIME: 20 MINUTES**
**TOTAL TIME: 2 HOURS AND 45 MINUTES**

Sweet balsamic and a touch of anise from the basil gives these wings depth.

## INGREDIENTS

12 fresh basil leaves, bruised

2 garlic cloves, crushed

2 teaspoons Dijon mustard

1 cup olive oil

¼ cup balsamic vinegar

1 tablespoon black pepper

1 tablespoon kosher salt

2 lbs. chicken wings

1. Place all of the ingredients, except for the chicken wings, in a mixing bowl or a plastic bag and stir until combined. Place the chicken wings in the marinade and chill in the refrigerator for at least 2 hours, stirring or shaking occasionally.

2. Remove the chicken wings from the refrigerator, remove them from the marinade, and shake to remove any excess. Spray the air fryer's basket with cooking spray and set it aside.

3. Place the wings in the basket so that they are not touching. Set the air fryer to 360°F and cook for 12 minutes. Turn the chicken wings over and cook for another 12 minutes. Raise the heat to 390°F, cook until the wings are extremely crispy, about 6 minutes, and serve.

# Wings in Citrus Marinade

**YIELD: 6 SERVINGS** • **ACTIVE TIME: 20 MINUTES**
**TOTAL TIME: 2 HOURS AND 45 MINUTES**

Plenty of citrus and cilantro guarantees that your wings will be bursting with vibrant flavors.

**1.** Place all of the ingredients, except for the chicken wings, in a mixing bowl or a plastic bag and stir until combined. Place the chicken wings in the marinade and chill in the refrigerator for at least 2 hours, stirring or shaking occasionally.

**2.** Remove the chicken wings from the refrigerator, remove them from the marinade, and shake to remove any excess. Spray the air fryer's basket with cooking spray and set it aside.

**3.** Place the wings in the basket so that they are not touching. Set the air fryer to 360°F and cook for 12 minutes. Turn the chicken wings over and cook for another 12 minutes. Raise the heat to 390°F, cook until the wings are extremely crispy, about 6 minutes, and serve.

## INGREDIENTS

¾ cup orange juice

Juice from ½ lime

Juice from ½ lemon

¼ cup chopped fresh cilantro

¼ cup olive oil

2 sprigs of fresh rosemary

4 garlic cloves, chopped

1 tablespoon black pepper

1 tablespoon kosher salt

2 lbs. chicken wings

# *Carolina Chicken Wings*

---

**YIELD: 6 SERVINGS • ACTIVE TIME: 20 MINUTES**
**TOTAL TIME: 2 HOURS AND 45 MINUTES**

---

This marinade looks to the rich BBQ tradition present in the Carolinas for inspiration.

*1.* Place all of the ingredients, except for the chicken wings, in a mixing bowl or a plastic bag and stir until combined. Place the chicken wings in the marinade and chill in the refrigerator for at least 2 hours, stirring or shaking occasionally.

*2.* Remove the chicken wings from the refrigerator, remove them from the marinade, and shake to remove any excess. Spray the air fryer's basket with cooking spray and set it aside.

*3.* Place the wings in the basket so that they are not touching. Set the air fryer to 360°F and cook for 12 minutes. Turn the chicken wings over and cook for another 12 minutes. Raise the heat to 390°F, cook until the wings are extremely crispy, about 6 minutes, and serve.

## INGREDIENTS

1 cup apple cider vinegar

2 tablespoons dark brown sugar

1 tablespoon olive oil

2 teaspoons Worcestershire sauce

2 teaspoons red pepper flakes

1 teaspoon paprika

1 teaspoon black pepper

1 teaspoon kosher salt

2 lbs. chicken wings

# Brown Sugar BBQ Wings

**YIELD: 6 SERVINGS • ACTIVE TIME: 20 MINUTES**
**TOTAL TIME: 2 HOURS AND 45 MINUTES**

There's a little bit of everything in this marinade.

1. Place all of the ingredients, except for the chicken wings, in a mixing bowl or a plastic bag and stir until combined. Place the chicken wings in the marinade and chill in the refrigerator for at least 2 hours, stirring or shaking occasionally.

2. Remove the chicken wings from the refrigerator, remove them from the marinade, and shake to remove any excess. Spray the air fryer's basket with cooking spray and set it aside.

3. Place the wings in the basket so that they are not touching. Set the air fryer to 360°F and cook for 12 minutes. Turn the chicken wings over and cook for another 12 minutes. Raise the heat to 390°F, cook until the wings are extremely crispy, about 6 minutes, and serve.

### INGREDIENTS

1½ cups light brown sugar

3 tablespoons apple cider vinegar

3 tablespoons water

2 teaspoons red pepper flakes

1 tablespoon Dijon mustard

1 teaspoon black pepper

1 teaspoon kosher salt

2 lbs. chicken wings

# Bourbon & Brown Sugar Wings

**YIELD: 6 SERVINGS • ACTIVE TIME: 20 MINUTES**
**TOTAL TIME: 2 HOURS AND 45 MINUTES**

The butter makes these already-indulgent wings even more so.

### INGREDIENTS

4 tablespoons unsalted butter

½ cup bourbon

½ cup brown sugar

¼ cup apple cider vinegar

1 teaspoon Dijon mustard

1 teaspoon black pepper

1 teaspoon kosher salt

2 lbs. chicken wings

*1.* Place all of the ingredients, except for the chicken wings, in a mixing bowl or a plastic bag and stir until combined. Place the chicken wings in the marinade and chill in the refrigerator for at least 2 hours, stirring or shaking occasionally.

*2.* Remove the chicken wings from the refrigerator, remove them from the marinade, and shake to remove any excess. Spray the air fryer's basket with cooking spray and set it aside.

*3.* Place the wings in the basket so that they are not touching. Set the air fryer to 360°F and cook for 12 minutes. Turn the chicken wings over and cook for another 12 minutes. Raise the heat to 390°F, cook until the wings are extremely crispy, about 6 minutes, and serve.

# Maple & Apple Cider Wings

**YIELD: 6 SERVINGS • ACTIVE TIME: 20 MINUTES**
**TOTAL TIME: 2 HOURS AND 45 MINUTES**

Experiment with different amounts of ketchup and maple syrup until this marinade is just to your taste.

*1.* Place all of the ingredients, except for the chicken wings, in a mixing bowl or a plastic bag and stir until combined. Place the chicken wings in the marinade and chill in the refrigerator for at least 2 hours, stirring or shaking occasionally.

*2.* Remove the chicken wings from the refrigerator, remove them from the marinade, and shake to remove any excess. Spray the air fryer's basket with cooking spray and set it aside.

*3.* Place the wings in the basket so that they are not touching. Set the air fryer to 360°F and cook for 12 minutes. Turn the chicken wings over and cook for another 12 minutes. Raise the heat to 390°F, cook until the wings are extremely crispy, about 6 minutes, and serve.

### INGREDIENTS

1 tablespoon olive oil

2 garlic cloves, chopped

¾ cup ketchup

1 cup apple cider

¼ cup maple syrup

2 tablespoons apple cider vinegar

1 teaspoon sweet paprika

1 teaspoon Worcestershire sauce

1 teaspoon black pepper

1 teaspoon kosher salt

2 lbs. chicken wings

# *Wings in Five-Spice Marinade*

**YIELD: 6 SERVINGS • ACTIVE TIME: 20 MINUTES**
**TOTAL TIME: 2 HOURS AND 45 MINUTES**

Your taste buds will welcome the hint of sesame oil here.

### INGREDIENTS

¾ cup soy sauce

¼ cup rice vinegar

2-inch piece of fresh ginger, peeled and chopped

2 teaspoons sesame oil

2 teaspoons five-spice powder

3 tablespoons olive oil

1 teaspoon black pepper

2 lbs. chicken wings

*1.* Place all of the ingredients, except for the chicken wings, in a mixing bowl or a plastic bag and stir until combined. Place the chicken wings in the marinade and chill in the refrigerator for at least 2 hours, stirring or shaking occasionally.

*2.* Remove the chicken wings from the refrigerator, remove them from the marinade, and shake to remove any excess. Spray the air fryer's basket with cooking spray and set it aside.

*3.* Place the wings in the basket so that they are not touching. Set the air fryer to 360°F and cook for 12 minutes. Turn the chicken wings over and cook for another 12 minutes. Raise the heat to 390°F, cook until the wings are extremely crispy, about 6 minutes, and serve.

# Lime & Cilantro Chicken Wings

**YIELD: 6 SERVINGS • ACTIVE TIME: 15 MINUTES**
**TOTAL TIME: 2 HOURS AND 15 MINUTES**

The flavor here is as refreshing as a Margarita in August.

*1.* Place all of the ingredients, except for the chicken wings, in a mixing bowl or a plastic bag and stir until combined. Place the chicken wings in the marinade and chill in the refrigerator for at least 2 hours, stirring or shaking occasionally.

*2.* Remove the chicken wings from the refrigerator, remove them from the marinade, and shake to remove any excess. Spray the air fryer's basket with cooking spray and set it aside.

*3.* Place the wings in the basket so that they are not touching. Set the air fryer to 360°F and cook for 12 minutes. Turn the chicken wings over and cook for another 12 minutes. Raise the heat to 390°F, cook until the wings are extremely crispy, about 6 minutes, and serve.

### INGREDIENTS

Juice from 3 limes

½ cup olive oil

¼ cup chopped fresh cilantro

2 garlic cloves, minced

2 teaspoons black pepper

2 teaspoons kosher salt

1 teaspoon honey

2 lbs. chicken wings

# Spicy South Asian Chicken Wings

**YIELD: 6 SERVINGS • ACTIVE TIME: 20 MINUTES**
**TOTAL TIME: 2 HOURS AND 45 MINUTES**

Sambal oelek is an Indonesian chili paste, and the rest of the elements in this marinade capture the familiar flavors of Thai cuisine.

*1.* Place all of the ingredients, except for the chicken wings, in a mixing bowl or a plastic bag and stir until combined. Place the chicken wings in the marinade and chill in the refrigerator for at least 2 hours, stirring or shaking occasionally.

*2.* Remove the chicken wings from the refrigerator, remove them from the marinade, and shake to remove any excess. Spray the air fryer's basket with cooking spray and set it aside.

*3.* Place the wings in the basket so that they are not touching. Set the air fryer to 360°F and cook for 12 minutes. Turn the chicken wings over and cook for another 12 minutes. Raise the heat to 390°F, cook until the wings are extremely crispy, about 6 minutes, and serve.

## INGREDIENTS

2 bird's eye chili peppers

½ cup soy sauce

½ cup sambal oelek

1 tablespoon fish sauce

Juice from 3 limes

¼ cup brown sugar

1-inch piece of fresh ginger, peeled and chopped

2 lbs. chicken wings

# Tandoori Chicken Wings

**YIELD: 6 SERVINGS • ACTIVE TIME: 20 MINUTES
TOTAL TIME: 2 HOURS AND 45 MINUTES**

The longer you wait here, the better. In fact, don't hesitate to let the wings sit in the marinade overnight.

*1.* Place all of the ingredients, except for the chicken wings, in a mixing bowl or a plastic bag and stir until combined. Place the chicken wings in the marinade and chill in the refrigerator for at least 2 hours, stirring or shaking occasionally.

*2.* Remove the chicken wings from the refrigerator, remove them from the marinade, and shake to remove any excess. Spray the air fryer's basket with cooking spray and set it aside.

*3.* Place the wings in the basket so that they are not touching. Set the air fryer to 360°F and cook for 12 minutes. Turn the chicken wings over and cook for another 12 minutes. Raise the heat to 390°F, cook until the wings are extremely crispy, about 6 minutes, and serve.

## INGREDIENTS

2 tablespoons olive oil

2 garlic cloves, chopped

½ teaspoon turmeric

2 tablespoons cumin

1-inch piece of fresh ginger, peeled and minced

1 teaspoon paprika

1 teaspoon coriander seeds, crushed

3 tablespoons finely chopped fresh cilantro

Juice from ½ small lime

1½ cups plain yogurt

2 lbs. chicken wings

# Chipotle & Adobo Chicken Wings

**YIELD: 6 SERVINGS • ACTIVE TIME: 15 MINUTES**
**TOTAL TIME: 2 HOURS AND 15 MINUTES**

Chipotles in adobo are the rare canned good one can enjoy with no misgivings.

### INGREDIENTS

2 (7 oz.) cans of chipotle peppers in adobo

2 garlic cloves, chopped

Juice from 1 lime

1 teaspoon black pepper

1 teaspoon kosher salt

2 lbs. chicken wings

*1.* Place all of the ingredients, except for the chicken wings, in a food processor and blitz until combined. Pour the marinade into a mixing bowl or a plastic bag. Place the chicken wings in the marinade and chill in the refrigerator for at least 2 hours, stirring or shaking occasionally.

*2.* Remove the chicken wings from the refrigerator, remove them from the marinade, and shake to remove any excess. Spray the air fryer's basket with cooking spray and set it aside.

*3.* Place the wings in the basket so that they are not touching. Set the air fryer to 360°F and cook for 12 minutes. Turn the chicken wings over and cook for another 12 minutes. Raise the heat to 390°F, cook until the wings are extremely crispy, about 6 minutes, and serve.

## INGREDIENTS

1 onion, chopped

4 scallions, trimmed and chopped

2 scotch bonnet peppers, chopped

½ cup soy sauce

1 tablespoon white vinegar

½ cup olive oil

1 sprig of fresh thyme

2 teaspoons sugar

1 teaspoon kosher salt

1 teaspoon black pepper

1 teaspoon allspice

½ teaspoon grated fresh nutmeg

½ teaspoon cinnamon

2 lbs. chicken wings

# Wings in Jerk Marinade

Letting your chicken wings soak up Jamaica's signature flavor is one of the best decisions one can make in a kitchen.

*1.* Place all of the ingredients, except for the chicken wings, in a mixing bowl or a plastic bag and stir until combined. Place the chicken wings in the marinade and chill in the refrigerator for at least 2 hours, stirring or shaking occasionally.

*2.* Remove the chicken wings from the refrigerator, remove them from the marinade, and shake to remove any excess. Spray the air fryer's basket with cooking spray and set it aside.

*3.* Place the wings in the basket so that they are not touching. Set the air fryer to 360°F and cook for 12 minutes. Turn the chicken wings over and cook for another 12 minutes. Raise the heat to 390°F, cook until the wings are extremely crispy, about 6 minutes, and serve.

# Mojo Chicken Wings

YIELD: 6 SERVINGS • ACTIVE TIME: 20 MINUTES
TOTAL TIME: 2 HOURS AND 45 MINUTES

Based off a popular chicken recipe in Cuba, this marinade is both bright and fiery.

*1.* Place all of the ingredients, except for the chicken wings, in a food processor and blitz until combined. Pour the marinade into a mixing bowl or a plastic bag, add the chicken wings, and chill in the refrigerator for at least 2 hours, stirring or shaking occasionally.

*2.* Remove the chicken wings from the refrigerator, remove them from the marinade, and shake to remove any excess. Spray the air fryer's basket with cooking spray and set it aside.

*3.* Place the wings in the basket so that they are not touching. Set the air fryer to 360°F and cook for 12 minutes. Turn the chicken wings over and cook for another 12 minutes. Raise the heat to 390°F, cook until the wings are extremely crispy, about 6 minutes, and serve.

## INGREDIENTS

1 yellow onion, chopped

10 garlic cloves, peeled and chopped

2 scotch bonnet peppers, stemmed, seeds and ribs removed

½ cup chopped fresh cilantro

1 teaspoon dried thyme

1 tablespoon cumin

½ teaspoon allspice

1 cup orange juice

½ cup fresh lemon juice

½ teaspoon citric acid

Zest and juice of 1 lime

¼ cup olive oil

2 lbs. chicken wings

## INGREDIENTS

1 lemongrass stalk, trimmed and crushed

2 garlic cloves, chopped

1-inch piece of fresh ginger, peeled and minced

1 scallion, trimmed and chopped

¼ cup brown sugar

2 tablespoons gochujang paste

1 tablespoon sesame oil

1 tablespoon rice vinegar

¼ cup soy sauce

2 tablespoons fish sauce

1 tablespoon black pepper

2 lbs. chicken wings

# Korean Chicken Wings

For the most authentic flavor, do your best to track down the gochujang paste.

*1.* Place all of the ingredients, except for the chicken wings, in a mixing bowl or a plastic bag and stir until combined. Place the chicken wings in the marinade and chill in the refrigerator for at least 2 hours, stirring or shaking occasionally.

*2.* Remove the chicken wings from the refrigerator, remove them from the marinade, and shake to remove any excess. Spray the air fryer's basket with cooking spray and set it aside.

*3.* Place the wings in the basket so that they are not touching. Set the air fryer to 360°F and cook for 12 minutes. Turn the chicken wings over and cook for another 12 minutes. Raise the heat to 390°F, cook until the wings are extremely crispy, about 6 minutes, and serve.

# Vindaloo Wings

**YIELD: 6 SERVINGS • ACTIVE TIME: 20 MINUTES**
**TOTAL TIME: 2 HOURS AND 45 MINUTES**

Add as much cayenne pepper to this marinade as you can take—the flavor improves as the temperature rises.

*1.* Place all of the ingredients, except for the chicken wings, in a mixing bowl or a plastic bag and stir until combined. Place the chicken wings in the marinade and chill in the refrigerator for at least 2 hours, stirring or shaking occasionally.

*2.* Remove the chicken wings from the refrigerator, remove them from the marinade, and shake to remove any excess. Spray the air fryer's basket with cooking spray and set it aside.

*3.* Place the wings in the basket so that they are not touching. Set the air fryer to 360°F and cook for 12 minutes. Turn the chicken wings over and cook for another 12 minutes. Raise the heat to 390°F, cook until the wings are extremely crispy, about 6 minutes, and serve.

## INGREDIENTS

1 tablespoon garam masala

1 teaspoon turmeric

2 teaspoons paprika

1 teaspoon mustard powder

2 tablespoons sugar

2 teaspoons cumin

1 teaspoon cayenne pepper, or to taste

½ cup red wine vinegar

¼ cup tomato paste

6 tablespoons olive oil

2 lbs. chicken wings

# Salsa Verde Wings

**YIELD: 6 SERVINGS • ACTIVE TIME: 15 MINUTES**
**TOTAL TIME: 2 HOURS AND 15 MINUTES**

The sweet, tart taste of tomatillos does wonders for a chicken wing.

## INGREDIENTS

8 tomatillos, husked, rinsed, and halved

1 plum tomato, halved

2 garlic cloves

1 shallot, halved

1 jalapeño pepper, stemmed, seeds and ribs removed, and halved

¼ cup olive oil

1 tablespoon kosher salt

1 tablespoon cumin

2 lbs. chicken wings

*1.* Place all of the ingredients, except for the chicken wings, in a food processor and blitz until combined. Pour the marinade into a mixing bowl or a plastic bag. Place the chicken wings in the marinade and chill in the refrigerator for at least 2 hours, stirring or shaking occasionally.

*2.* Remove the chicken wings from the refrigerator, remove them from the marinade, and shake to remove any excess. Spray the air fryer's basket with cooking spray and set it aside.

*3.* Place the wings in the basket so that they are not touching. Set the air fryer to 360°F and cook for 12 minutes. Turn the chicken wings over and cook for another 12 minutes. Raise the heat to 390°F, cook until the wings are extremely crispy, about 6 minutes, and serve.

# Citrus & Jalapeño Wings

**YIELD: 6 SERVINGS • ACTIVE TIME: 20 MINUTES**
**TOTAL TIME: 2 HOURS AND 45 MINUTES**

If you're looking for more heat here, leave the ribs on the jalapeño and add its seeds as well.

1. Place all of the ingredients, except for the chicken wings, in a mixing bowl or a plastic bag and stir until combined. Place the chicken wings in the marinade, and chill in the refrigerator for at least 2 hours, stirring or shaking occasionally.

2. Remove the chicken wings from the refrigerator, remove them from the marinade, and shake to remove any excess. Spray the air fryer's basket with cooking spray and set it aside.

3. Place the wings in the basket so that they are not touching. Set the air fryer to 360°F and cook for 12 minutes. Turn the chicken wings over and cook for another 12 minutes. Raise the heat to 390°F, cook until the wings are extremely crispy, about 6 minutes, and serve.

### INGREDIENTS

½ cup orange juice

Juice of 1 lime

4 garlic cloves, chopped

1 jalapeño pepper, stemmed, seeds and ribs removed, and minced

2 tablespoons finely chopped fresh cilantro

1 teaspoon cumin

1 teaspoon dried oregano

Salt and pepper, to taste

¼ cup olive oil

2 lbs. chicken wings

# Garlic-Dijon Wings

**YIELD: 6 SERVINGS • ACTIVE TIME: 15 MINUTES**
**TOTAL TIME: 2 HOURS AND 15 MINUTES**

A bit of umami from the soy sauce bolsters this otherwise traditional marinade.

## INGREDIENTS

4 garlic cloves, chopped

3 tablespoons Dijon mustard

3 tablespoons soy sauce

3 tablespoons olive oil

3 tablespoons Worcestershire sauce

2 teaspoons black pepper

1 teaspoon kosher salt

2 lbs. chicken wings

*1.* Place all of the ingredients, except for the chicken wings, in a mixing bowl or a plastic bag and stir until combined. Place the chicken wings in the marinade and chill in the refrigerator for at least 2 hours, stirring or shaking occasionally.

*2.* Remove the chicken wings from the refrigerator, remove them from the marinade, and shake to remove any excess. Spray the air fryer's basket with cooking spray and set it aside.

*3.* Place the wings in the basket so that they are not touching. Set the air fryer to 360°F and cook for 12 minutes. Turn the chicken wings over and cook for another 12 minutes. Raise the heat to 390°F, cook until the wings are extremely crispy, about 6 minutes, and serve.

## INGREDIENTS

½ cup olive oil

¼ cup red wine vinegar

Juice of 2 lemons

2 teaspoons cinnamon

2 tablespoons coriander

1 tablespoon black pepper

1 teaspoon cardamom

1 teaspoon ground cloves

½ teaspoon mace

Pinch of ground nutmeg

1 tablespoon garlic powder

½ teaspoon kosher salt

1 teaspoon sumac powder

2 lbs. chicken wings

# Shawarma Wings

**YIELD: 6 SERVINGS • ACTIVE TIME: 20 MINUTES
TOTAL TIME: 2 HOURS AND 45 MINUTES**

Some pita bread and hummus will be lovely flanking these wings.

*1.* Place all of the ingredients, except for the chicken wings, in a mixing bowl or a plastic bag and stir until combined. Place the chicken wings in the marinade and chill in the refrigerator for at least 2 hours, stirring or shaking occasionally.

*2.* Remove the chicken wings from the refrigerator, remove them from the marinade, and shake to remove any excess. Spray the air fryer's basket with cooking spray and set it aside.

*3.* Place the wings in the basket so that they are not touching. Set the air fryer to 360°F and cook for 12 minutes. Turn the chicken wings over and cook for another 12 minutes. Raise the heat to 390°F, cook until the wings are extremely crispy, about 6 minutes, and serve.

# Crying Tiger Wings

**YIELD: 6 SERVINGS • ACTIVE TIME: 20 MINUTES**
**TOTAL TIME: 2 HOURS AND 45 MINUTES**

Don't be afraid—the tears these wings will produce are those of joy.

## INGREDIENTS

2 tablespoons soy sauce

1 tablespoon oyster sauce

2 tablespoons brown sugar

$\frac{1}{3}$ cup fresh lime juice

$\frac{1}{4}$ cup fish sauce

2 tablespoons finely chopped fresh cilantro

2 tablespoons finely chopped fresh basil

1 tablespoon red pepper flakes

2 tablespoons finely chopped fresh mint

2 lbs. chicken wings

1. Place all of the ingredients, except for the chicken wings, in a mixing bowl or a plastic bag and stir until combined. Place the chicken wings in the marinade and chill in the refrigerator for at least 2 hours, stirring or shaking occasionally.

2. Remove the chicken wings from the refrigerator, remove them from the marinade, and shake to remove any excess. Spray the air fryer's basket with cooking spray and set it aside.

3. Place the wings in the basket so that they are not touching. Set the air fryer to 360°F and cook for 12 minutes. Turn the chicken wings over and cook for another 12 minutes. Raise the heat to 390°F, cook until the wings are extremely crispy, about 6 minutes, and serve.

Bask in the unique buzz supplied by Sichuan peppercorns.

*1.* Place all of the ingredients, except for the chicken wings, in a food processor and blitz until combined. Pour the marinade into a mixing bowl or a plastic bag. Place the chicken wings in the marinade and chill in the refrigerator for at least 2 hours, stirring or shaking occasionally.

*2.* Remove the chicken wings from the refrigerator, remove them from the marinade, and shake to remove any excess. Spray the air fryer's basket with cooking spray and set it aside.

*3.* Place the wings in the basket so that they are not touching. Set the air fryer to 360°F and cook for 12 minutes. Turn the chicken wings over and cook for another 12 minutes. Raise the heat to 390°F, cook until the wings are extremely crispy, about 6 minutes, and serve.

## INGREDIENTS

1 tablespoon cumin seeds, crushed

3 tablespoons Sichuan peppercorns, crushed

¼ cup olive oil

¼ cup sesame oil

1 yellow onion, sliced

2 scallions, trimmed and sliced thin

1 teaspoon kosher salt

4 whole dried red chili peppers

2 teaspoons red pepper flakes

2 lbs. chicken wings

# Wings in Savory Citrus Marinade

**YIELD: 6 SERVINGS • ACTIVE TIME: 15 MINUTES**
**TOTAL TIME: 2 HOURS AND 15 MINUTES**

Soy sauce, coriander, and cumin give this otherwise light marinade some backbone.

## INGREDIENTS

Juice from 2 limes

4 garlic cloves, minced

¾ cup orange juice

1 cup chopped fresh cilantro

1 tablespoon soy sauce

1 teaspoon coriander

2 teaspoons cumin

1 tablespoon kosher salt

1 tablespoon black pepper

¼ cup olive oil

2 lbs. chicken wings

*1.* Place all of the ingredients, except for the chicken wings, in a mixing bowl or a plastic bag and stir until combined. Place the chicken wings in the marinade and chill in the refrigerator for at least 2 hours, stirring or shaking occasionally.

*2.* Remove the chicken wings from the refrigerator, remove them from the marinade, and shake to remove any excess. Spray the air fryer's basket with cooking spray and set it aside.

*3.* Place the wings in the basket so that they are not touching. Set the air fryer to 360°F and cook for 12 minutes. Turn the chicken wings over and cook for another 12 minutes. Raise the heat to 390°F, cook until the wings are extremely crispy, about 6 minutes, and serve.

# Wings in All-Purpose Marinade

**YIELD: 6 SERVINGS • ACTIVE TIME: 20 MINUTES**
**TOTAL TIME: 2 HOURS AND 45 MINUTES**

A standard marinade for those times when you can't leave anything to chance.

*1.* Place all of the ingredients, except for the chicken wings, in a mixing bowl or a plastic bag and stir until combined. Place the chicken wings in the marinade and chill in the refrigerator for at least 2 hours, stirring or shaking occasionally.

*2.* Remove the chicken wings from the refrigerator, remove them from the marinade, and shake to remove any excess. Spray the air fryer's basket with cooking spray and set it aside.

*3.* Place the wings in the basket so that they are not touching. Set the air fryer to 360°F and cook for 12 minutes. Turn the chicken wings over and cook for another 12 minutes. Raise the heat to 390°F, cook until the wings are extremely crispy, about 6 minutes, and serve.

## INGREDIENTS

½ cup soy sauce

3 tablespoons Worcestershire sauce

2 garlic cloves, minced

¼ onion, minced

¼ cup olive oil

Juice from 1 lime

2 lbs. chicken wings

# Garlic & Fennel Wings

**YIELD: 6 SERVINGS • ACTIVE TIME: 20 MINUTES**
**TOTAL TIME: 2 HOURS AND 45 MINUTES**

Fans of fennel are in for a treat here.

### INGREDIENTS

8 garlic cloves, minced

1 tablespoon cumin

2 tablespoons black pepper

3 tablespoons fennel seeds, crushed

1 tablespoon paprika

2 tablespoons kosher salt

2 teaspoons Dijon mustard

1 cup olive oil

2 lbs. chicken wings

*1.* Place all of the ingredients, except for the chicken wings, in a mixing bowl or a plastic bag and stir until combined. Place the chicken wings in the marinade and chill in the refrigerator for at least 2 hours, stirring or shaking occasionally.

*2.* Remove the chicken wings from the refrigerator, remove them from the marinade, and shake to remove any excess. Spray the air fryer's basket with cooking spray and set it aside.

*3.* Place the wings in the basket so that they are not touching. Set the air fryer to 360°F and cook for 12 minutes. Turn the chicken wings over and cook for another 12 minutes. Raise the heat to 390°F, cook until the wings are extremely crispy, about 6 minutes, and serve.

# Rosemary-Balsamic Wings

**YIELD: 6 SERVINGS • ACTIVE TIME: 20 MINUTES
TOTAL TIME: 2 HOURS AND 45 MINUTES**

Sweet and sharp, these wings make quite an impression.

*1.* Place all of the ingredients, except for the chicken wings, in a mixing bowl or a plastic bag and stir until combined. Place the chicken wings in the marinade and chill in the refrigerator for at least 2 hours, stirring or shaking occasionally.

*2.* Remove the chicken wings from the refrigerator, remove them from the marinade, and shake to remove any excess. Spray the air fryer's basket with cooking spray and set it aside.

*3.* Place the wings in the basket so that they are not touching. Set the air fryer to 360°F and cook for 12 minutes. Turn the chicken wings over and cook for another 12 minutes. Raise the heat to 390°F, cook until the wings are extremely crispy, about 6 minutes, and serve.

### INGREDIENTS

1 cup balsamic vinegar

¼ cup olive oil

2 sprigs of fresh rosemary

Salt and pepper, to taste

2 lbs. chicken wings

# Scintillating Sauces

This chapter is all about options. Aside from Buffalo Wings (see page 137), where doctrine dictates that the sauce be applied after the wings have been cooked, you get to decide what direction you'll take once the sauce has been prepared. You can use the following preparations on the side for dipping, toss the chicken wings in the chosen sauce before or after frying, or use them as a marinade or baste, armed in each instance with the knowledge that they will always be delicious.

# Buffalo Wings

**YIELD: 6 SERVINGS · ACTIVE TIME: 10 MINUTES
TOTAL TIME: 35 MINUTES**

The sauce that lifted the humble chicken wing onto menus all over the world.

*1.* Spray the air fryer's basket with cooking spray and set it aside. Season the chicken wings with salt and pepper and set them aside.

*2.* Place the butter in a saucepan and melt over medium heat. Stir in the vinegar, hot sauce, and cayenne, making sure not to breathe in the spicy steam, transfer the sauce to a mixing bowl, and cover it with aluminum foil.

*3.* Place the wings in the basket so that they are not touching. Set the air fryer to 360°F and cook for 12 minutes. Turn the chicken wings over and cook for another 12 minutes. Raise the heat to 390°F, cook until the wings are extremely crispy, about 6 minutes. Toss the chicken wings in the sauce until coated and serve with the Blue Cheese Sauce and celery sticks.

## INGREDIENTS

2 lbs. chicken wings

Salt and pepper, to taste

4 tablespoons unsalted butter

1 tablespoon white vinegar

¾ cup hot sauce

1 teaspoon cayenne pepper

Blue Cheese Sauce
(see page 191), for serving

Celery sticks, for serving

# *Fermented Hot Sauce*

**YIELD: 2 CUPS • ACTIVE TIME: 10 MINUTES**
**TOTAL TIME: 30 DAYS TO 6 MONTHS**

If you're a hot sauce addict, this homemade offering will take that addiction to the next level.

*1.* Remove the tops of the peppers and split them down the middle.

*2.* Place the split peppers and the garlic, onion, and salt in a mason jar and cover with water. Cover the jar and shake well.

*3.* Place the jar away from direct sunlight and let stand for a minimum of 30 days, and up to 6 months. The flavor will improve the longer the mixture ferments.

*4.* Once you are ready to make the sauce, reserve the brine, transfer the solids to a blender, and puree to desired thickness. If you want your sauce to be on the thin side, keep adding brine until you have the consistency you want. Season with salt, transfer to a container, cover, and store in the refrigerator for up to 3 months.

## INGREDIENTS

2 lbs. cayenne peppers

1 lb. jalapeño peppers

5 garlic cloves, chopped

1 red onion, quartered

3 tablespoons kosher salt, plus more to taste

Filtered water, as needed

# Black Strap BBQ Sauce

A healthy dose of molasses grounds this beguiling sauce.

*1.* Place all of the ingredients in a saucepan, stir to combine, and bring to a boil over medium-high heat. Reduce the heat to medium and cook until the sauce has reduced by one-third, about 20 minutes. Taste, adjust the seasoning if necessary, and use as desired.

**INGREDIENTS**

½ cup ketchup

¼ cup dark brown sugar

2 tablespoons granulated sugar

2 tablespoons Dijon mustard

3 tablespoons apple cider vinegar

2 garlic cloves, minced

¼ cup blackstrap molasses

¼ teaspoon ground cloves

½ teaspoon hot sauce

¼ cup honey

# Smoky Southern BBQ Sauce

**YIELD: 1½ CUPS • ACTIVE TIME: 30 MINUTES**
**TOTAL TIME: 1½ HOURS**

A touch of smoke fills this sauce with intense flavor.

*1.* An hour before grilling, soak the woodchips in a bowl of water.

*2.* Preheat a gas or charcoal grill to medium-high heat (about 450°F).

*3.* Place the garlic, onion, tomatoes, and tomato paste in a food processor and blitz until combined. Add the remaining ingredients and blitz until incorporated. Pour the sauce into a saucepan.

*4.* When the grill is ready, drain the woodchips and spread them over the coals or pour them into a smoker box. Place the saucepan on the grill and then bring the sauce to a boil with the grill covered. Let the sauce cook until it has reduced by about one-third, about 20 minutes. Taste, adjust the seasoning if necessary, and use as desired.

## INGREDIENTS

1 cup hickory or oak woodchips

2 garlic cloves, minced

1 white onion, minced

1 cup crushed tomatoes

¼ cup tomato paste

2 tablespoons white wine vinegar

2 tablespoons balsamic vinegar

1 tablespoon Dijon mustard

Juice from 1 lime

1-inch piece of fresh ginger, peeled and minced

1 teaspoon smoked paprika

½ teaspoon cinnamon

2 dried chipotle peppers, seeded and minced

1 habanero pepper, stemmed, seeds and ribs removed, and minced (optional)

Salt and pepper, to taste

# Maple BBQ Sauce

YIELD: 1½ CUPS • ACTIVE TIME: 15 MINUTES
TOTAL TIME: 35 MINUTES

The sweetness of the maple syrup works beautifully with savory chicken wings.

**1.** Place the olive oil in a saucepan and warm over medium-high heat. When the oil starts to shimmer, add the onion and garlic and cook until the onion is translucent, about 3 minutes.

**2.** Stir in the remaining ingredients and bring the sauce to a boil. Reduce the heat to medium and simmer until the sauce has reduced by one-third, about 20 minutes. Taste, adjust the seasoning if necessary, and use as desired.

### INGREDIENTS

2 tablespoons olive oil

¼ white onion, minced

2 garlic cloves, minced

1 cup ketchup

3 tablespoons apple cider vinegar

1 tablespoon unsalted butter

½ cup real maple syrup

2 tablespoons molasses

2 teaspoons mustard powder

Salt and pepper, to taste

# Apple & Mustard BBQ Sauce

YIELD: 1½ CUPS • ACTIVE TIME: 15 MINUTES
TOTAL TIME: 35 MINUTES

However you decide to use this sweet and smoky sauce, make sure you're generous with it.

## INGREDIENTS

1 tablespoon olive oil

½ shallot, minced

½ cup apple cider

½ cup white wine vinegar

1 tablespoon tequila

2 teaspoon finely chopped fresh parsley

2 tablespoons fish sauce

1 tablespoon honey

1 tablespoon Dijon mustard

2 teaspoons spicy mustard

Salt and pepper, to taste

*1.* Place the olive oil in a saucepan and warm over medium-high heat. When the oil starts to shimmer, add the shallot and cook until it is translucent, about 3 minutes.

*2.* Stir in the remaining ingredients and bring the sauce to a boil. Reduce the heat to medium and simmer until the sauce has reduced by one-third, about 20 minutes. Taste, adjust the seasoning if necessary, and use as desired.

## INGREDIENTS

1 tablespoon olive oil

4 garlic cloves, minced

1 cup ketchup

¼ cup water

2 tablespoons molasses

2 tablespoons
dark brown sugar

1 tablespoon
apple cider vinegar

1 tablespoon
Worcestershire sauce

1 bay leaf

1 teaspoon mustard powder

1 teaspoon chili powder

1 teaspoon onion powder

1 teaspoon liquid smoke

1 teaspoon black pepper

1 teaspoon kosher salt

# *Kansas City BBQ Sauce*

**YIELD: 1½ CUPS • ACTIVE TIME: 10 MINUTES**
**TOTAL TIME: 15 MINUTES**

BBQ is a major source of regional pride, and this sauce makes it easy to understand why the folks in Kansas City believe their version to be the best.

*1.* Place the olive oil in a saucepan and warm over medium heat. When it starts to shimmer, add the garlic and cook until it starts to turn golden brown, about 2 minutes.

*2.* Stir in the remaining ingredients and bring to a boil. Reduce the heat to medium and simmer until the sauce has reduced by one-third, about 20 minutes.

*3.* Remove the bay leaf and discard it. Taste the sauce, adjust the seasoning if necessary, and use as desired.

# South Carolina BBQ Sauce

**YIELD: 2 CUPS • ACTIVE TIME: 5 MINUTES
TOTAL TIME: 30 MINUTES**

The mustard adds a lovely tangy quality to this sauce, ensuring that its flavor lingers in the mind long after the meal is done.

*1.* Place all of the ingredients in a saucepan, stir to combine, and bring to a boil over medium-high heat. Reduce the heat to medium and cook until the sauce has reduced by one-third, about 20 minutes.

*2.* Taste, adjust the seasoning if necessary, and use as desired.

### INGREDIENTS

1 cup yellow mustard

½ cup honey

½ cup apple cider vinegar

2 tablespoons ketchup

1 tablespoon light brown sugar

2 teaspoons Worcestershire sauce

3 garlic cloves, minced

1 teaspoon ground black pepper

Salt, to taste

# *Charred Peach BBQ Sauce*

**YIELD: 2 CUPS • ACTIVE TIME: 15 MINUTES**
**TOTAL TIME: 30 MINUTES**

Peaches may seem out of place on your grill, but the resulting char brings out their best.

*1.* Preheat a gas or charcoal grill to medium-high heat (about 450°F). When the grill is ready, place the peaches, cut-side down, on the grill. Cook until they are charred and starting to caramelize, about 6 minutes. Remove from the grill and let the peaches cool slightly. Place them in a food processor, blitz until pureed, and set aside.

*2.* Place the olive oil in a saucepan and warm over medium heat. When it starts to shimmer, add the onion and garlic and cook until the onion turns translucent, about 3 minutes.

*3.* Stir in the remaining ingredients and the peach puree and bring to a boil. Reduce the heat to medium and simmer until the sauce has reduced by one-third, about 20 minutes.

*4.* Taste, adjust the seasoning if necessary, and use as desired.

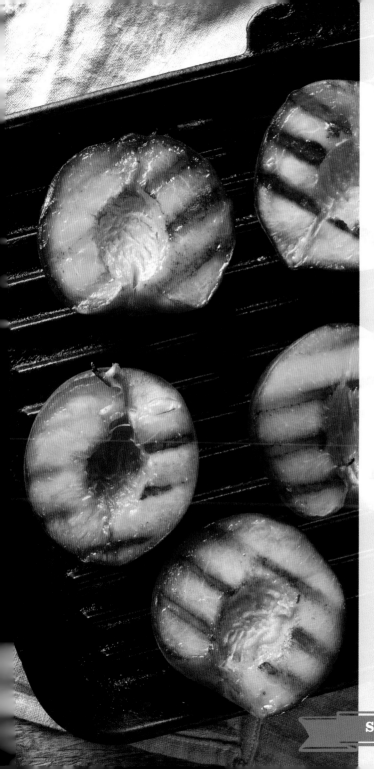

## INGREDIENTS

4 peaches, halved and pitted

2 tablespoons olive oil

1 small onion, minced

4 garlic cloves, minced

1 cup pureed tomatoes

½ cup ketchup

¼ cup light brown sugar

¼ cup molasses

2 tablespoons honey

1 tablespoon Worcestershire sauce

2 tablespoons peach preserves

Juice from ½ lemon

1 teaspoon black pepper

1 teaspoon kosher salt

# St. Louis BBQ Sauce

The molasses, brown sugar, and apple cider vinegar and slow cooking combine to make a rich sauce that will help your wings take off.

1. Place all of the ingredients in a saucepan, stir to combine, and bring to a boil over medium-high heat. Reduce the heat to medium-low and cook for 1 hour, stirring occasionally.

2. Taste, adjust the seasoning if necessary, and use as desired.

## INGREDIENTS

2 cups pureed tomatoes

2 tablespoons Dijon mustard

¼ cup apple cider vinegar

¼ cup molasses

1 cup dark brown sugar

1 teaspoon Worcestershire sauce

2 garlic cloves, minced

1 teaspoon black pepper

1 teaspoon kosher salt

# Honey & Bourbon BBQ Sauce

**YIELD: 1½ CUPS • ACTIVE TIME: 10 MINUTES**
**TOTAL TIME: 35 MINUTES**

If you prefer to maximize the sweet character of this sauce, simply omit the liquid smoke.

## INGREDIENTS

2 tablespoons olive oil

4 garlic cloves, minced

1 cup ketchup

½ cup bourbon

3 tablespoons honey

2 tablespoons brown sugar

1 tablespoon soy sauce

1 tablespoon Worcestershire sauce

1 tablespoon Dijon mustard

1 teaspoon liquid smoke

1 teaspoon black pepper

1 teaspoon kosher salt

*1.* Place the olive oil in a saucepan and warm over medium heat. When it starts to shimmer, add the garlic and cook until it starts to turn golden brown, about 2 minutes.

*2.* Stir in the remaining ingredients and bring to a boil. Reduce the heat to medium and simmer until the sauce has reduced by one-third, about 20 minutes.

*3.* Taste the sauce, adjust the seasoning if necessary, and use as desired.

# Coffee & Bourbon BBQ Sauce

**YIELD: 2 CUPS • ACTIVE TIME: 5 MINUTES**
**TOTAL TIME: 30 MINUTES**

A marriage of the Texan and Southern BBQ traditions, where the slight bitterness of the coffee and sweet bourbon work in perfect harmony.

*1.* Place all of the ingredients in a saucepan, stir to combine, and bring to a boil over medium-high heat. Reduce the heat to medium and simmer until the sauce has reduced by one-third, about 20 minutes.

*2.* Taste, adjust the seasoning if necessary, and use as desired.

## INGREDIENTS

2 cups brewed coffee

¼ cup dark brown sugar

¾ cup bourbon

3 tablespoons molasses

¼ cup apple cider vinegar

2 tablespoons Worcestershire sauce

¼ cup ketchup

1 tablespoon granulated garlic

½ tablespoon black pepper

1 tablespoon cornstarch

# Smoky Stout BBQ Sauce

**YIELD: 2 CUPS • ACTIVE TIME: 5 MINUTES**
**TOTAL TIME: 30 MINUTES**

Stout has a slightly bitter, chocolaty quality that goes perfectly with the sweetness and smokiness here.

### INGREDIENTS

1 cup Guinness or preferred stout

1 cup ketchup

½ cup apple cider vinegar

½ cup gently packed dark brown sugar

2 tablespoons honey

2 tablespoons Worcestershire sauce

1 teaspoon liquid smoke

1 teaspoon black pepper

1 teaspoon kosher salt

*1.* Place all of the ingredients in a saucepan, stir to combine, and bring to a boil over medium-high heat. Reduce the heat to medium and cook until the sauce has reduced by one-third, about 20 minutes.

*2.* Taste, adjust the seasoning if necessary, and use as desired.

# Universal BBQ Sauce

**YIELD: 2 CUPS • ACTIVE TIME: 10 MINUTES**
**TOTAL TIME: 40 MINUTES**

Looking for a sauce that is certain to satisfy everyone? This one has you covered.

## INGREDIENTS

1¼ cups ketchup

1 cup gently packed dark brown sugar

¼ cup molasses

¼ cup apple cider vinegar

¼ cup water

1 tablespoon Worcestershire sauce

2 teaspoons mustard powder

2 teaspoons garlic powder

2 teaspoons smoked paprika

¼ teaspoon cayenne pepper

Salt and pepper, to taste

1 tablespoon all-purpose flour

**1.** Place all of the ingredients, except for the flour, in a saucepan, stir to combine, and bring to a boil over medium-high heat. Reduce the heat to medium and cook until the sauce has reduced by one-third, about 20 minutes.

**2.** Gradually incorporate the flour and stir constantly to prevent lumps from forming. Simmer for 5 minutes, taste the sauce, adjust the seasoning if necessary, and use as desired.

# Korean BBQ Sauce

YIELD: 1 CUP • ACTIVE TIME: 10 MINUTES
TOTAL TIME: 30 MINUTES

Should this sauce not meet your expectations, try cutting the amount of ketchup until it's right.

## INGREDIENTS

½ cup soy sauce

¼ cup ketchup

¼ cup rice wine vinegar

3 tablespoons light brown sugar

2 teaspoons gochujang paste

2 garlic cloves, minced

1 teaspoon sesame oil

½-inch piece of fresh ginger, peeled and grated

4 scallions, trimmed and chopped

1 teaspoon black pepper

*1.* Place all of the ingredients in a saucepan, stir to combine, and bring to a boil over medium-high heat. Reduce the heat to medium and cook until the sauce has reduced by one-third, about 20 minutes.

*2.* Taste, adjust the seasoning if necessary, and use as desired.

# Basil Pesto

If you want a chunkier pesto—or don't have a food processor—use a knife to chop up the ingredients.

*1.* Place the pine nuts in a dry skillet and toast them over medium heat, shaking the skillet frequently, until they start to turn golden brown. Transfer the pine nuts to a bowl and let cool.

*2.* Place the pine nuts, basil leaves, shallot, and garlic in a food processor and pulse until the mixture is a thick paste. Gradually incorporate the olive oil until you reach the desired consistency.

*3.* Place the mixture in a bowl, stir in the Parmesan, season with salt and pepper, and use as desired.

## INGREDIENTS

½ cup pine nuts

3 cups fresh basil leaves

¼ small shallot

2 garlic cloves

½ cup olive oil

¼ cup grated Parmesan cheese

Salt and pepper, to taste

# Sun-Dried Tomato Pesto

YIELD: 1¼ CUPS • ACTIVE TIME: 5 MINUTES
TOTAL TIME: 5 MINUTES

If you purchase sun-dried tomatoes that aren't in olive oil, make sure you soak them in boiling water for 10 minutes before draining and incorporating them into the sauce.

## INGREDIENTS

12 sun-dried tomatoes in olive oil, drained

½ cup fresh basil leaves

½ small shallot

¼ cup blanched almonds

1 garlic clove

½ cup olive oil

Salt and pepper, to taste

*1.* Place all of the ingredients, except for the olive oil, in a food processor and pulse until the mixture is a thick paste.

*2.* Gradually incorporate the olive oil until you reach the desired consistency. Place the mixture in a bowl, season with salt and pepper, and use as desired.

# Creamy Garlic & Chive Sauce

**YIELD: 1¼ CUPS • ACTIVE TIME: 2 MINUTES**
**TOTAL TIME: 2 MINUTES**

A standard topping for a baked potato will also serve you well beside a plate of hot wings.

### INGREDIENTS

1 cup sour cream

6 garlic cloves, minced

¼ cup finely chopped fresh chives

Juice from ½ lemon

Salt and pepper, to taste

*1.* Place all of the ingredients in a bowl, stir until combined, and use as desired.

# *Hot Honey Mustard*

YIELD: 1½ CUPS • ACTIVE TIME: 2 MINUTES
TOTAL TIME: 2 MINUTES

A classic dipping sauce for wings, with an added kick.

## INGREDIENTS

1 cup mayonnaise

¼ cup Dijon mustard

¼ cup Hot Honey
(see opposite page)

2 tablespoons fresh
lemon juice

Salt, to taste

*1.* Place all of the ingredients in a bowl, stir until combined, and use as desired.

# Hot Honey

**YIELD: 1 CUP • ACTIVE TIME: 10 MINUTES**
**TOTAL TIME: 2 HOURS**

This is a key part of the Hot Honey Mustard on the opposite page, but it's also great in its own right.

**1.** Place the chili peppers and honey in a saucepan and bring to a very gentle simmer over medium-low heat. Reduce heat to lowest possible setting and cook for 1 hour.

**2.** Remove the saucepan from heat and let the mixture infuse for another hour.

**3.** Remove the peppers. Transfer the honey to a container, cover, and store in the refrigerator.

**INGREDIENTS**

4 hot chili peppers

1 cup honey

**NOTE:** FRESNO AND CAYENNE PEPPERS WILL PRODUCE THE BEST RESULTS.

# Spicy Mango Chutney

**YIELD: 1½ CUPS • ACTIVE TIME: 10 MINUTES**
**TOTAL TIME: 30 MINUTES**

A beautiful balance of sweetness and spice that will serve you well.

*1.* Place all of the ingredients in a saucepan and stir to combine. Bring to a boil over medium-high heat, reduce the heat to medium, and simmer until the mixture acquires a jam-like consistency, about 20 minutes. If a smoother consistency is desired, mash the mangoes as they cook.

*2.* Remove the pan from heat, let the chutney cool completely, and use as desired.

### INGREDIENTS

2 large mangoes, peeled, pitted, and diced

1 cup white vinegar

¾ cup sugar

1 large red onion, chopped

2-inch piece of fresh ginger, peeled and minced

1 teaspoon cayenne pepper

1 teaspoon mustard seeds, crushed

2 garlic cloves, chopped

1 teaspoon kosher salt

# Sesame & Sriracha Sauce

By taking a little something from a number of Asian cuisines, this sauce enters a world of its own.

*1.* Place the olive oil in a large skillet and warm over medium-high heat. When it starts to shimmer, add the onion, garlic, and ginger and sauté until the onion is translucent, about 3 minutes.

*2.* Add the sesame oil, soy sauce, stock, sriracha, and sugar to the skillet and bring to a boil over medium-high heat. Reduce the heat to low and simmer until the sauce has reduced by one-third, about 20 minutes.

*3.* Stir in the cornstarch and water and cook the sauce until it thickens slightly, about 2 minutes. Taste, adjust the seasoning if necessary, and use as desired.

## INGREDIENTS

2 tablespoons olive oil

1 small onion, chopped

3 garlic cloves, minced

2-inch piece of fresh ginger, peeled and minced

1½ teaspoons toasted sesame oil

3 tablespoons soy sauce

1 cup chicken stock

2 tablespoons sriracha, or to taste

3 tablespoons sugar

2 teaspoons cornstarch

1 teaspoon water

# *Green Goddess Sauce*

The divine moniker is no accident—this sauce is robust but also delicate enough to keep you mindful of the fresh herbs that produced it.

## INGREDIENTS

½ cup mayonnaise

2/3 cup buttermilk

1 tablespoon fresh lemon juice

2 tablespoons finely chopped celery leaves

2 tablespoons finely chopped fresh parsley

1 teaspoon black pepper

2 tablespoons finely chopped fresh tarragon

2 tablespoons finely chopped fresh chives

2 teaspoons kosher salt

*1.* Place all of the ingredients in a food processor, blitz until combined, and use as desired.

# Romesco Sauce

This red pepper–based sauce originated in the fishing villages of Catalonia, but its bold, zippy flavor has since carried it onto tables across the globe.

*1.* Place all of the ingredients, except for the olive oil, in a food processor and blitz until combined.

*2.* Gradually incorporate the olive oil and blitz until emulsified. Taste, adjust the seasoning if necessary, and use as desired.

## INGREDIENTS

2 large roasted red bell peppers

1 garlic clove, smashed

½ cup slivered almonds, toasted

¼ cup tomato puree

2 tablespoons finely chopped fresh parsley

2 tablespoons sherry vinegar

1 teaspoon smoked paprika

Salt and pepper, to taste

½ cup olive oil

# Sofrito

**YIELD: 2 CUPS • ACTIVE TIME: 10 MINUTES**
**TOTAL TIME: 10 MINUTES**

A versatile sauce that is key to a number of beloved dishes in the Caribbean.

## INGREDIENTS

2 poblano peppers, stemmed and seeds and ribs removed

1 red onion, peeled and cut into quarters

1 red bell pepper, stemmed and seeds and ribs removed

1 green bell pepper, stemmed and seeds and ribs removed

3 plum tomatoes

2 garlic cloves

1 tablespoon cumin

2 tablespoons adobo seasoning

¼ cup finely chopped fresh parsley

¼ cup finely chopped fresh cilantro

1. Dice 1 of the poblanos, half of the onion, and half of each of the bell peppers. Set them aside.

2. Place the rest of the ingredients in a blender or food processor and blitz until smooth. Transfer the puree to a bowl and stir in the diced vegetables. Taste, adjust the seasoning if necessary, and use as desired.

# Takoyaki Sauce

An easy-to-prepare option that delivers a breathtaking blast of umami.

*1.* Place all of the ingredients in a small bowl and stir to combine. Taste, adjust the seasoning if necessary, and use as desired.

**INGREDIENTS**

1 cup Worcestershire sauce

2 tablespoons mentsuyu

1½ tablespoons honey

1 tablespoon ketchup

# Gingery Red Pepper Sauce

**YIELD: 1 CUP • ACTIVE TIME: 5 MINUTES**
**TOTAL TIME: 25 MINUTES**

The sweet and velvety appearance belies the kick provided by the ginger.

### INGREDIENTS

3 red bell peppers, stemmed, seeds and ribs removed, and chopped

2-inch piece of fresh ginger, peeled and chopped

4 garlic cloves

¼ cup sugar

3 tablespoons tomato paste

2 tablespoons olive oil

2 tablespoons apple cider vinegar

2 tablespoons soy sauce

*1.* Place all of the ingredients in a food processor and blitz until pureed.

*2.* Place the puree in a saucepan and cook, stirring occasionally, over medium heat until the sauce has achieved the desired consistency and flavor, about 20 minutes. Strain and use as desired.

# Marinara Sauce

**YIELD: 2 CUPS • ACTIVE TIME: 20 MINUTES**
**TOTAL TIME: 2 HOURS**

Every great cook needs a foolproof marinara, as there remains no better method to capture the flavor of fresh tomatoes.

**1.** Place all of the ingredients, except for the basil and parsley, in a saucepan and cook, stirring frequently, over medium heat until the tomatoes begin to break down, about 10 minutes. Reduce the heat to low and cook, stirring occasionally, for about 1 1/2 hours, or until the flavor is to your liking.

**2.** Stir in the basil and parsley and season to taste. The sauce will be chunky. If you prefer a smoother texture, transfer the sauce to a blender or food processor and puree before using as desired.

## INGREDIENTS

½ lb. tomatoes, quartered

¼ small yellow onion, sliced

2 garlic cloves, crushed

¼ teaspoon finely chopped fresh thyme

¼ teaspoon finely chopped fresh oregano

1 tablespoon olive oil

Salt and pepper, to taste

2 teaspoons finely chopped fresh basil

1 teaspoon finely chopped fresh parsley

# Spicy Tomato Sauce

**YIELD: 2 CUPS • ACTIVE TIME: 15 MINUTES**
**TOTAL TIME: 45 MINUTES**

A recipe for those times when you want a little something more alongside the sweetness of tomatoes.

## INGREDIENTS

1 spicy chili pepper

2 tablespoons olive oil

1 small shallot, minced

2 garlic cloves, minced

½ lb. tomatoes, crushed

2 tablespoons finely chopped fresh cilantro

1 teaspoon finely chopped fresh parsley

2 teaspoons finely chopped fresh chives

Salt and pepper, to taste

*1.* Preheat the broiler to high and place the chili on a baking sheet. Broil, turning the pepper occasionally, until it is charred and blistered all over. Remove from the oven and let cool. When the chili is cool enough to handle, remove the stem and seeds, discard them, mince the flesh, and set aside.

*2.* Place the olive oil in a saucepan and warm over medium heat. When the oil starts to shimmer, add the shallot and garlic and sauté for 2 minutes. Stir in the chili, add the tomatoes, and cook until they start to break down, about 10 minutes.

*3.* Stir in the cilantro, parsley, and chives and cook until the flavor has developed to your liking. Season with salt and pepper and serve.

# *Blue Cheese Sauce*

Any blue cheese will do here, but don't be afraid to switch it up and try different varieties.

*1.* Place the mayonnaise, sour cream, and vinegar in a mixing bowl and stir until combined. Stir in the blue cheese and chives, season with salt and pepper, and use as desired.

### INGREDIENTS

¾ cup mayonnaise

½ cup sour cream

2 tablespoons white wine vinegar

½ lb. blue cheese, crumbled

3 tablespoons finely chopped fresh chives

Salt and pepper, to taste

# Easy Aioli

**YIELD: 2 CUPS • ACTIVE TIME: 5 MINUTES**
**TOTAL TIME: 5 MINUTES**

Excellence doesn't get any easier.

## INGREDIENTS

1½ cups mayonnaise

6 garlic cloves, minced

3 tablespoons fresh lemon juice

2 tablespoons smooth Dijon mustard

Salt and pepper, to taste

*1.* Place all of the ingredients in a mixing bowl and stir to combine. Taste, adjust the seasoning if necessary, and use as desired.

# Chipotle Sauce

YIELD: 2 CUPS • ACTIVE TIME: 5 MINUTES
TOTAL TIME: 5 MINUTES

The mayonnaise and sour cream provide a soft landing spot for the bold flavor of the chipotles.

*1.* Place all of the ingredients in a mixing bowl and stir to combine. Taste, adjust the seasoning if necessary, and use as desired.

### INGREDIENTS

1 cup pureed tomatoes

3 tablespoons fresh lime juice

3 scallions, trimmed and chopped

3 garlic cloves, minced

3 chipotle chili peppers in adobo, minced

1 teaspoon adobo sauce

Salt, to taste

# Apple & Hoisin Dipping Sauce

This will be lovely with any of the spicier wings.

**INGREDIENTS**

¾ cup unsweetened applesauce

½ cup hoisin sauce

¼ cup firmly packed dark brown sugar

6 tablespoons ketchup

2 tablespoons honey

2 tablespoons rice wine vinegar

1 tablespoon soy sauce

1 tablespoon chili garlic sauce, or to taste

*1.* Place all of the ingredients in a mixing bowl and stir to combine. Taste, adjust the seasoning if necessary, and use as desired.

# Spicy Peanut Sauce

YIELD: 2 CUPS • ACTIVE TIME: 10 MINUTES
TOTAL TIME: 10 MINUTES

The recommendation for chunky peanut butter is far from law—if you're a devotee of smooth PB, by all means use it here.

## INGREDIENTS

1 cup chunky peanut butter

½ cup hot water (125°F)

½ cup firmly packed dark brown sugar

⅓ cup fresh lime juice

¼ cup soy sauce

2 tablespoons sesame oil

2 tablespoons chili garlic sauce

6 garlic cloves, minced

3 scallions, trimmed and chopped

¼ cup chopped fresh cilantro

*1.* Place the peanut butter, water, brown sugar, lime juice, soy sauce, sesame oil, and chili garlic sauce in a mixing bowl and stir to combine. Stir in the garlic, scallions, and cilantro. Taste, adjust the seasoning if necessary, and use as desired.

# Yakisoba Sauce

**YIELD: 1½ CUPS • ACTIVE TIME: 10 MINUTES**
**TOTAL TIME: 45 MINUTES**

The sauce used to power the beloved Japanese street food gets broken out to stunning effect.

### INGREDIENTS

3 tablespoons sake

3 tablespoons mirin

3 tablespoons soy sauce

3 tablespoons oyster sauce

3 tablespoons Worcestershire sauce

¼ cup sugar

Salt and white pepper, to taste

¼ cup ketchup

*1.* Place all of the ingredients, except for the ketchup, in a saucepan and bring to a simmer over medium heat, stirring to dissolve the sugar.

*2.* When the sugar has dissolved, stir in the ketchup and remove the pan from heat. Let the sauce cool completely and then use as desired.

# Side Dishes

If you're just having a snack, then the chicken wing recipes by themselves will treat you well. But if you're looking to make them part of an actual meal, you'll need to flank them with one or more of the delicious sides featured in this chapter.

## INGREDIENTS

2½ cups milk

2½ cups chicken stock

2 cups medium-grain cornmeal

2 tablespoons unsalted butter

1 teaspoon kosher salt, plus more to taste

½ teaspoon black pepper

½ teaspoon dried oregano

½ teaspoon dried thyme

½ teaspoon dried rosemary

Vegetable oil, as needed

¼ cup grated Parmesan cheese, for garnish

2 tablespoons finely chopped fresh rosemary, for garnish

# *Polenta Fries*

The beautiful golden hue of these fries looks great alongside chicken wings.

*1.* Grease a large, rimmed baking sheet with cooking spray. Place the milk and stock in a saucepan and bring to a boil. Whisk in the cornmeal, reduce the heat to low and cook, stirring constantly, until all of the liquid has been absorbed and the mixture is creamy, about 5 minutes.

*2.* Stir in the butter, salt, pepper, oregano, thyme, and rosemary. When they have been incorporated, transfer the polenta to the greased baking sheet and even out the surface with a rubber spatula. Refrigerate for 2 hours.

*3.* Carefully invert the baking sheet over a cutting board so that the polenta falls onto it. Slice in half lengthwise and cut each piece into 4-inch-long and 1-inch-wide strips.

*4.* Add oil to a Dutch oven until it is approximately 2 inches deep and bring it to 375°F. Working in batches of two, place the strips in the oil and fry, turning as they cook, until golden brown, 2 to 4 minutes. Transfer the cooked fries to a paper towel–lined plate to drain. When all of the fries have been cooked, sprinkle the Parmesan and rosemary over them and serve.

# *Thai Fried Rice*

**YIELD: 4 SERVINGS • ACTIVE TIME: 35 MINUTES**
**TOTAL TIME: 1 HOUR**

The directions call for kohlrabi and peas, but you can include any vegetable you like.

**1.** Place the rice and water in a saucepan, cover it, and simmer for 20 minutes. Remove from heat, fluff with a fork, and let cool, uncovered, so that the rice dries out a little. Set it aside.

**2.** Place 1 tablespoon of the oil in a large skillet and warm over medium-high heat. When it starts to shimmer, add the shallot, kohlrabi, peas, and ginger and sauté until the kohlrabi is tender and the peas are cooked through, about 8 minutes. Remove the mixture from the pan and set it aside.

**3.** Add the rice to the pan. It is very likely that the rice will stick to the bottom. Do your best to scrape it off with a spatula. Cook the rice until it starts to brown, about 5 to 10 minutes, taking care not to let it become too mushy. Add the soy sauce and rice vinegar and stir to incorporate.

**4.** Add the pineapple, cashews, and the kohlrabi mixture. Gently fold to incorporate and cook for another |minute to heat everything through. Season to taste, garnish with the cilantro, and serve.

## INGREDIENTS

1 cup jasmine rice

2 cups water

2 tablespoons olive oil, plus more as needed

1 shallot, diced

1 kohlrabi, peeled and diced

½ cup frozen peas

1-inch piece of fresh ginger, peeled and minced

1 tablespoon soy sauce

1 tablespoon rice vinegar

½ cup diced pineapple

¼ cup cashews

¼ cup finely chopped fresh cilantro, for garnish

# Coconut & Cucumber Salad

**YIELD: 6 SERVINGS • ACTIVE TIME: 30 MINUTES**
**TOTAL TIME: 40 MINUTES**

A great way to cool down the spicier wings in the book.

## INGREDIENTS

5 large cucumbers, peeled, halved lengthwise, and seeded

½ cup shredded unsweetened coconut

Zest and juice of 2 limes

¼ cup coconut milk

1 teaspoon chili garlic sauce, plus more to taste

½-inch piece of fresh ginger, peeled and grated

1 teaspoon sugar

1 teaspoon cumin

1 teaspoon kosher salt, plus more to taste

½ cup roasted peanuts, chopped, for serving

6 scallions, trimmed and sliced thin, for serving

1. Quarter each cucumber half and then cut the quarters into long, ⅛-inch-wide strips. Place the strips on paper towels to drain.

2. Place the coconut, lime juice, coconut milk, chili garlic sauce, ginger, sugar, cumin, and salt in a food processor and blitz until smooth.

3. Place the cucumbers in a large serving bowl. Top with the coconut mixture and toss to coat.

4. Sprinkle the lime zest, peanuts, and scallions on top of the dressed noodles, season to taste, and serve immediately.

# *Herbed Potato Salad*

The tangy vinaigrette lets the natural sweetness of the potatoes come through.

## INGREDIENTS

1½ lbs. new or red potatoes, cubed

½ cup olive oil

3 tablespoons white wine vinegar

2 tablespoons dry white wine

1 teaspoon whole-grain Dijon mustard

1 teaspoon kosher salt, plus more to taste

1 shallot, minced

Black pepper, to taste

2 tablespoons finely chopped fresh parsley

2 tablespoons finely chopped fresh chives

2 tablespoons finely chopped fresh dill

*1.* Add the potatoes to a pot large enough to hold them all, cover with water, bring to a boil, reduce heat, and simmer until tender, about 15 minutes.

*2.* While the potatoes are simmering, whisk together the oil, vinegar, wine, mustard, and salt.

*3.* When the potatoes are done, drain and place them in a bowl. Add the vinaigrette and shallot immediately and gently toss, making sure to coat all of the potatoes. Let the salad cool completely.

*4.* Taste and adjust seasoning as needed. Season with salt and pepper, stir in the fresh herbs, and serve.

# Dry-Fried Beans

**YIELD: 4 SERVINGS • ACTIVE TIME: 30 MINUTES**
**TOTAL TIME: 45 MINUTES**

If you can't find Chinese pickled vegetables, sauerkraut or kimchi will also work.

**1.** Place the oil in a large sauté pan and warm over high heat. When it starts to shimmer, add the green beans and cook, without stirring, until they start to char, about 6 minutes. Turn the beans over and cook until they are browned all over, about 5 minutes. Transfer to a bowl and set aside.

**2.** Add the pickled vegetables and the garlic to the pan and sauté until fragrant, about 2 minutes. Stir in the sherry and cook until it has nearly evaporated. Stir in the soy sauce, fermented black bean garlic sauce, and sugar and return the green beans to the pan. Cook until heated through and serve.

## INGREDIENTS

1 tablespoon olive oil, plus more as needed

1 lb. green beans, trimmed

2 tablespoons chopped Chinese pickled vegetables

1 garlic clove, chopped

2 tablespoons sherry

2 tablespoons soy sauce

1 tablespoon fermented black bean garlic sauce

1 teaspoon sugar

# Corn Bread

**YIELD: 16 SERVINGS • ACTIVE TIME: 40 MINUTES**
**TOTAL TIME: 2 HOURS AND 15 MINUTES**

Incorporating a creamy corn puree into the batter makes all the difference in a homemade corn bread.

## INGREDIENTS

5 ears of corn, silk removed

10 tablespoons unsalted butter

1 cup diced onion

3 garlic cloves, minced

2 teaspoons kosher salt, plus more to taste

2¾ cups heavy cream

2 cups all-purpose flour

2 cups cornmeal

¼ cup brown sugar

½ teaspoon paprika

2 tablespoons baking powder

½ teaspoon cayenne pepper

1½ cups honey

6 eggs

¼ cup sour cream

*1.* Preheat the oven to 400°F.

*2.* Place the ears of corn on a baking sheet, place them in the oven, and bake for 25 minutes, until the kernels have a slight give to them. Remove from the oven and let cool. When the ears of corn are cool enough to handle, remove the husks and cut the kernels from the cobs. Lower the oven temperature to 300°F.

*3.* Place 2 tablespoons of the butter in a large saucepan and melt over medium heat. Add the onion and garlic, season with salt, and sauté until the onion is translucent, about 3 minutes. Set ³/₄ cup of the corn kernels aside and add the rest to the pan. Add 2 cups of the cream and a pinch of salt and cook until the corn is very tender, about 15 to 20 minutes.

**4.** Strain, reserve the cream, and transfer the solids to the blender. Puree until smooth, adding the cream as needed. Season to taste and let the puree cool completely.

**5.** Place the flour, cornmeal, remaining salt, brown sugar, paprika, baking powder, and cayenne pepper in a large mixing bowl and stir until combined. Place 2 cups of the corn puree, the honey, eggs, remaining cream, and the sour cream in a separate large mixing bowl and stir until combined. Gradually add the dry mixture to the wet mixture and stir to combine. When all of the dry mixture has been incorporated, add the reserved corn kernels and fold to incorporate them.

**6.** Grease an 11 x 7–inch baking pan and pour in the batter into it. Place the corn bread in the oven and bake until a toothpick inserted into the center comes out clean, about 35 minutes. Remove from the oven and let cool slightly before serving.

# *Musaengchae*

A traditional Korean side dish that is capable of freshening up any table it appears on.

*1.* Place all of the ingredients in a mixing bowl and stir to combine. Let marinate for 1 hour at room temperature before serving.

**INGREDIENTS**

2 cups shredded daikon radish

2 cucumbers, sliced thin

1 teaspoon gochujang powder

2 tablespoons rice vinegar

1 tablespoon kosher salt

1 tablespoon sugar

# Retro Bread & Butter Pickles

**YIELD: 4 SERVINGS • ACTIVE TIME: 5 MINUTES**
**TOTAL TIME: 3 HOURS**

A refreshing blast from the past.

## INGREDIENTS

**5 Persian cucumbers, sliced thin**

**1 small onion, sliced thin**

**2 jalapeño peppers, stemmed, seeds and ribs removed, and sliced thin**

**4 sprigs of fresh dill**

**2 tablespoons coriander seeds, crushed**

**2 tablespoons mustard seeds, crushed**

**2 teaspoons celery salt**

**2 cups distilled white vinegar**

**1 cup sugar**

**2 tablespoons kosher salt**

*1.* Place the cucumbers, onion, jalapeños, dill, coriander seeds, mustard seeds, and celery salt in a sterilized 1-quart mason jar.

*2.* Place the vinegar, sugar, and salt in a medium saucepan and bring it to a boil, while stirring to dissolve the sugar and salt. Carefully pour the brine into jar, filling all the way to the top. Let cool completely before sealing and storing in the refrigerator, where they will keep for up to 1 week.

# Zucchini Fritters

**YIELD: 4 SERVINGS • ACTIVE TIME: 15 MINUTES**
**TOTAL TIME: 30 MINUTES**

A great spot for the surfeit of zucchini summer seems to bring.

**INGREDIENTS**

1½ lbs. zucchini

Salt and pepper, to taste

¼ cup all-purpose flour

¼ cup grated
Parmesan cheese

1 egg, beaten

3 tablespoons olive oil

*1.* Line a colander with cheesecloth and grate the zucchini into the colander. Generously sprinkle salt over the zucchini, stir to combine, and let sit for 1 hour. After 1 hour, press down on the zucchini to remove as much liquid from it as you can.

*2.* Place the zucchini, flour, Parmesan, and egg in a mixing bowl and stir to combine. Form handfuls of the mixture into balls and then gently press down on the balls to flatten them into patties.

*3.* Place the oil in a cast-iron skillet and warm over medium-high heat. Working in batches, place the patties in the oil, taking care not to crowd the skillet. Cook until golden brown, about 5 minutes. Flip them over and cook for another 5 minutes, until the fritters are also golden brown on that side. Remove from the skillet, transfer to a paper towel–lined plate, and repeat with the remaining patties. When all of the fritters have been cooked, season with salt and pepper and serve.

# Kale Chips

YIELD: 4 SERVINGS  •  ACTIVE TIME: 10 MINUTES
TOTAL TIME: 30 MINUTES

Get some green beside those wings and any guilt over indulging will evaporate.

*1.* Preheat the oven to 350°F. Tear the kale leaves into smaller pieces and place them in a mixing bowl. Add the remaining ingredients and work the mixture with your hands until the kale is evenly coated.

*2.* Divide the seasoned kale between 2 parchment-lined baking sheets so that it sits on each in an even layer. Place in the oven and bake until crispy, 6 to 8 minutes. Remove and let cool before serving.

## INGREDIENTS

1 bunch of kale, stems removed

1 teaspoon kosher salt

½ teaspoon black pepper

½ teaspoon paprika

½ teaspoon dried parsley

½ teaspoon dried basil

¼ teaspoon dried thyme

¼ teaspoon dried sage

2 tablespoons olive oil

# Kimchi

YIELD: 4 CUPS • ACTIVE TIME: 30 MINUTES
TOTAL TIME: 3 TO 7 DAYS

A lovely example of the wonders of fermentation.

**1.** Place the cabbage and salt in a large bowl and stir to combine. Wash your hands, or put on gloves, and work the mixture, squeezing to remove as much liquid as possible from the cabbage. Let the mixture rest for 2 hours.

**2.** Add the remaining ingredients, except for the water, work the mixture with your hands until well combined, and squeeze to remove as much liquid from the cabbage as possible.

**3.** Transfer the mixture to a large mason jar and press down so it is tightly packed. The liquid should be covering the mixture. If it is not, add water until the mixture is covered.

**4.** Cover the jar and let the mixture sit at room temperature for 3 to 7 days, removing the lid daily to release the gas that has built up.

## INGREDIENTS

1 head of napa cabbage, cut into strips

½ cup kosher salt

2-inch piece of fresh ginger, peeled and minced

3 garlic cloves, minced

1 teaspoon sugar

5 tablespoons red pepper flakes

3 bunches of scallions, trimmed and sliced

Water, as needed

# Blistered Shishito Peppers

**YIELD: 4 TO 6 SERVINGS • ACTIVE TIME: 5 MINUTES
TOTAL TIME: 10 MINUTES**

These peppers are a bit like putting your taste buds through a round of Russian roulette, since approximately one in every 10 is spicy, and there's no way to tell until you bite down. The rest are as mild as can be.

**INGREDIENTS**

Olive oil, as needed

2 lbs. shishito peppers

Salt, to taste

*1.* Add olive oil to a 12-inch cast-iron skillet until it is $1/4$ inch deep and warm over medium heat.

*2.* When the oil starts to shimmer, add the peppers and cook, while turning once or twice, until they are blistered and golden brown all over, about 8 minutes. Take care not to crowd the pan with the peppers, and work in batches if necessary.

*3.* Transfer the blistered peppers to a paper towel–lined plate, season with salt, and serve.

# Southern Collard Greens

When you think these greens are done, just keep cooking them.

**1.** Place the oil in a large saucepan over and warm over medium-high heat. When the oil starts to shimmer, add the onion and sauté until it is translucent, about 3 minutes. Add the ham, reduce heat to medium, and cook until the ham starts to brown, about 5 minutes.

**2.** Add the remaining ingredients, stir to combine, and cover the pan. Braise the collard greens until they are very tender, about 2 hours. Check on the collards every so often and add water if all of the liquid has evaporated.

## INGREDIENTS

2 tablespoons olive oil

1 onion, diced

½ lb. smoked ham, diced

4 garlic cloves, diced

3 lbs. collard greens, stems removed, chopped

2 cups chicken stock

¼ cup apple cider vinegar

1 tablespoon brown sugar

1 teaspoon red pepper flakes

# Onion Rings

YIELD: 4 SERVINGS • ACTIVE TIME: 15 MINUTES
TOTAL TIME: 20 MINUTES

A preparation that benefits from the air fryer almost as much as chicken wings.

## INGREDIENTS

½ cup all-purpose flour

Salt, to taste

½ teaspoon paprika

1 egg, beaten

½ cup buttermilk

1 cup panko

2 tablespoons olive oil

2 large yellow onions, sliced into thick rings

*1.* Place the flour, a pinch of salt, and the paprika in a shallow bowl and stir to combine. Place the egg and buttermilk in another bowl and stir to combine. Add ¼ cup of the flour mixture and stir until incorporated. Place the panko and olive oil in third bowl, stir until combined, and season with salt.

*2.* Spray the air fryer basket with cooking spray. Dredge the onions in the flour mixture, then in the egg mixture, and lastly in the panko mixture. Repeat until fully coated. Place the onion rings in the air fryer basket.

*3.* Cook at 400°F for 12 to 15 minutes, until the onion rings are crispy and golden brown. Carefully remove from the air fryer and serve.

# Stovetop Brussels Sprouts

**YIELD: 4 SERVINGS • ACTIVE TIME: 10 MINUTES
TOTAL TIME: 15 MINUTES**

The closer you can get these to burnt, the better they'll be.

**1.** Warm a large cast-iron skillet over high heat. When it begins to smoke, add all of the Brussels sprouts and a few tablespoons of water. Place the lid on and steam for 2 minutes.

**2.** Remove the lid and add enough oil to coat the bottom of the pan. Reduce heat to medium and let the Brussels sprouts brown, turning them occasionally until they are brown all over.

**3.** Continue cooking until the desired tenderness is achieved, adding more oil if the pan starts to look dry. Season with salt and pepper and serve.

## INGREDIENTS

1 lb. Brussels sprouts, trimmed and halved

Olive oil, as needed

Salt and pepper, to taste

# Basic Red Cabbage Slaw

**YIELD: 4 SERVINGS • ACTIVE TIME: 10 MINUTES**
**TOTAL TIME: 3 HOURS AND 10 MINUTES**

Incredibly easy, but the cabbage needs time with the salt to become tender.

## INGREDIENTS

1 small red cabbage, cored and sliced as thin as possible

1 teaspoon kosher salt, plus more to taste

Juice of 1 lime

1 bunch of fresh cilantro, chopped

*1.* Place the cabbage in a large bowl, sprinkle the salt on top, and toss to distribute. Use your hands to work the salt into the cabbage, then let the mixture sit for 3 hours.

*2.* Once it has rested, taste to gauge the saltiness: if too salty, rinse under cold water and let drain; if just right, add the lime juice and cilantro, stir to combine, and serve.

# Home-Style Baked Beans

**YIELD: 6 SERVINGS • ACTIVE TIME: 30 MINUTES**
**TOTAL TIME: 1½ HOURS**

Images of cowboys and campfires will be dancing in your head thanks to these baked beans.

*1.* Preheat the oven to 325°F. Warm a large cast-iron skillet over medium heat and add the bacon. Cook until it is crispy, about 3 minutes. Transfer the bacon to a paper towel–lined plate.

*2.* Add the onion and bell pepper to the skillet and sauté until the vegetables start to soften, about 5 minutes.

*3.* Stir in the salt, beans, BBQ sauce, mustard, and brown sugar. Bring to a simmer, season with salt and pepper, and then return the bacon to the pan.

*4.* Transfer the skillet to the oven. Bake for about 1 hour, until the sauce is thick and the flavor has developed to your liking. Remove from the oven and let the beans cool slightly before serving.

### INGREDIENTS

3 strips of thick-cut bacon, chopped

½ onion, diced

½ cup diced bell pepper

1 teaspoon kosher salt, plus more to taste

2 (14 oz.) cans of pinto beans, drained and rinsed

1 cup BBQ sauce

1 teaspoon Dijon mustard

2 tablespoons dark brown sugar

Black pepper, to taste

# Metric Equivalents

## Weights

| | |
|---|---|
| 1 ounce | 28 grams |
| 2 ounces | 57 grams |
| 4 ounces (¼ pound) | 113 grams |
| 8 ounces (½ pound) | 227 grams |
| 16 ounces (1 pound) | 454 grams |

## Volume Measures

| | | |
|---|---|---|
| ⅛ teaspoon | | 0.6 ml |
| ¼ teaspoon | | 1.23 ml |
| ½ teaspoon | | 2.5 ml |
| 1 teaspoon | | 5 ml |
| 1 tablespoon (3 teaspoons) | ½ fluid ounce | 15 ml |
| 2 tablespoons | 1 fluid ounce | 29.5 ml |
| ¼ cup (4 tablespoons) | 2 fluid ounces | 59 ml |
| ⅓ cup (5⅓ tablespoons) | 2.7 fluid ounces | 80 ml |
| ½ cup (8 tablespoons) | 4 fluid ounces | 120 ml |
| ⅔ cup (10⅔ tablespoons) | 5.4 fluid ounces | 160 ml |
| ¾ cup (12 tablespoons) | 6 fluid ounces | 180 ml |
| 1 cup (16 tablespoons) | 8 fluid ounces | 240 ml |

## Temperature Equivalents

| °F | °C | Gas Mark |
|---|---|---|
| 225 | 110 | ¼ |
| 250 | 130 | ½ |
| 275 | 140 | 1 |
| 300 | 150 | 2 |
| 325 | 170 | 3 |
| 350 | 180 | 4 |
| 375 | 190 | 5 |
| 400 | 200 | 6 |
| 425 | 220 | 7 |
| 450 | 230 | 8 |
| 475 | 240 | 9 |
| 500 | 250 | 10 |

## Length Measures

| | |
|---|---|
| ¹⁄₁₆-inch | 1.6 mm |
| ⅛-inch | 3 mm |
| ¼-inch | 0.63 cm |
| ½-inch | 1.25 cm |
| ¾-inch | 2 cm |
| 1-inch | 2.5 cm |

# Index

# ABOUT CIDER MILL PRESS BOOK PUBLISHERS

Good ideas ripen with time. From seed to harvest, Cider Mill Press brings fine reading, information, and entertainment together between the covers of its creatively crafted books. Our Cider Mill bears fruit twice a year, publishing a new crop of titles each spring and fall.

"Where Good Books Are Ready for Press"

Visit us online at
cidermillpress.com
or write to us at
PO Box 454
12 Spring St.
Kennebunkport, Maine 04046